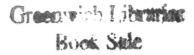

The Modern Coarse Angler

by

DAVE KING

Edited by
COLIN DYSON

PUBLICATIONS

First published in Great Britain by
Pisces Angling Publications
P.O. Box 116, Doncaster
South Yorkshire DN5 9NH

First Published — April 1986

ISBN 0 948584 02 5 (hardback)
ISBN 0 948584 03 3 (softback)

Printed by Jackson Wilson Ltd.,
24 Jack Lane, Leeds LS11 5NB
Typesetting/Design by Three's Company — Leeds

Further copies available from:—
Pisces Angling Publications

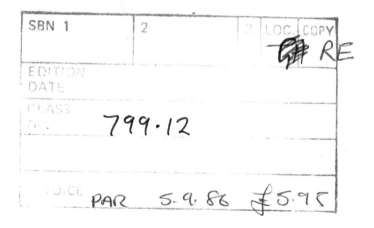

PUBLICATIONS

CONTENTS

FOREWORD

Writing a book for angling beginners is a task many professional angling writers would avoid, and I have to include myself. It is the most difficult job I can think of, partly because the knowledgeable angler finds it awfully boring to return to the basics — even if he can remember what the basics really are!

Through my involvement with Coarse Angler magazine, and especially with an advice column in Anglers Mail, I know how very easy it is to write over the heads of some of the readers. No matter how simple the advice there is nearly always something — some reference to a method or even just a single word — which the reader does not know or cannot understand.

As we acquire knowledge it degenerates into jargon. We talk and write in a kind of shorthand, comprehensible only to those who are roughly on the same level. Baffled youngsters, and beginners of all ages, are excluded from the 'club', often too embarrased to seek enlightenment for fear of making fools of themselves.

There are many fine books which enable competent anglers to get better, either as all rounders or specialists in a particular field, but pitifully few which can really help the beginner become competent. The one I used, in my period as an embryo angler was, I grew up to learn, a very sketchy effort indeed.

Dave King is a character the sport is all too short of. Before ill health curtailed his activities he had progressed as a good all-round angler, with a good match fishing record at club and local open match level. He also got himself involved with teaching youngsters at schools and youth clubs, exposing himself to those questions which too often remain unasked.

He could not find a beginners' book which answered all those questions, and he began to write one himself, scribbling notes between calls on a salesmans round! A brave venture for an untrained writer. I haven't asked how long it took him, but I do know he has ended up with something worthwhile.

Great literature it certainly isn't. Neither I nor anyone else could have made it so with a complete re-write, let alone the minor tinkering with the manuscript which I was able to do to help him. The subject doesn't lend itself to a work of art, but he's done what I suspect few if any professional angling writers could have achieved. He has got right down to basics and dealt with details and problems which all experienced anglers have forgotten they ever had.

I hope he won't mind me putting it this way, but a measure of his success is that some passages bored me to distraction, in the same way that 'O' level mathematics would bore a computer expert. But that's exactly how it had to be with a book which aims to bridge the yawning gap which lies between beginner's and the level of competence they all hope to achieve.

This book will get them there a lot quicker than most, and new generations of anglers will have cause to thank Dave King — not just for tackling the awesome job of writing it, but also for having the courage to risk publishing it himself.

Colin Dyson.

Author demonstrates shotting to a young angler.

INTRODUCTION

Many books have been written about angling, and many more will be written as long as angling methods continue to progress and be developed, and as our understanding of the habits and environment of the quarry is increased.

Many of the excellent modern specialist books written by successful and established specimen anglers, are, or will become, the bibles of all thinking anglers who wish to, and have the "ability" to progress into this very advanced and rewarding side of angling. Modern match fishing is also blessed with men of oustanding ability as anglers and communicators in their craft.

In this age of modern fishery management and freedom of transport, anglers are no longer geographically constrained, and any angler with the will to progress and learn can follow his chosen path without restraint, providing he has served his apprenticeship well, and has been able to overcome most of the commercial and tackle handling pitfalls that lay in the path of all newcomers to the sport. His rate of development will depend largely upon whether he has been fortunate to be guided through the maze by a competent friend or relation, or has been able to interpret and put into practice much of the excellent information now available in the angling press.

Despite the availability of information, either verbal or written, I have found over the years with my involvement in angling education, that for every one reasonably competent or successful angler with the ability to progress into their chosen aspect of the sport, there are ten others who are still struggling to overcome the basic problems and to grasp the science of the sport. Many in fact have given up the struggle, and disillusioned with their lack of progress, have either left the sport to take up golf, or still go fishing for the benefit of the relaxation and peaceful surroundings (which is the reward of all anglers, competent or otherwise), and have resigned themselves to being fortunate if an occasional fish rewards their patience by allowing itself to be caught on a bait poorly or unnaturally presented.

Much of the blame for this is either on the part of the angler for being too proud to avail himself of the information now available, or on the part of the authors of the many introductory books and articles on angling, assuming too much knowledge to be already held by the reader in the way of basic tackle handling experience and watercraft. I have come across many novice anglers who stop fishing and pack up when it gets windy because they know from experience they will be unable to catch fish because their tackle will not stay where they want it to, and they are unable to control it.

I was once in this same position, and when an accomplished angler revealed to me the secret of sinking my line and altering my float and shotting to combat this "monumental handicap", I was so amazed and impressed that he ceased to be a mere mortal in my estimation. I remember as a lad how, when I fished with a fellow young angler on the Leicester Canal, he would be continually catching fish, whilst I, using the 'same' float, shotting and bait, would always remain fishless.

I consoled myself with the thought that he was "just one of those jammy devils", always dropping on a good swim. With a name like Roy Marlow, he wouldn't amount to very much anyway! Fortunately I was able to subdue this natural but negative attitude, and thanks to the help and guidance of such excellent mentors, and by reading the few decent books on angling that were available at that time, I was able to progress, and armed with this knowledge, eventually mastered most of the aspects of the sport.

This then is the aim of this book, to introduce tomorrow's match stars, specimen hunters and pleasure anglers to our sport and explain not only what to do, but also what not to do and help them achieve their ultimate ambitions:— to catch fish.

1 THE TACKLE SHOP

Most angling books start by describing types of fishing equipment but as you can see this one doesn't. It starts at the beginning, where most new followers of our sport start, at the window of the tackle shop. Before we go in let's have a think about what we are going in for.

The first thing we need from the tackle dealer is advice. To give advice a tackle dealer needs several important things. I will list them in what I consider to be the order of importance.

Firstly he needs to be an angler himself. Normally if the shop you have decided to go to is a specialist shop, i.e. it only sells fishing tackle, then this is normally an assurance that the owner is an angler. It does not always follow that the person behind the counter is. It may be the owner's wife or daughter, or just a shop assistant who is there to keep the shop open whilst the owner is out or preparing bait, in which case they may not be able to advise you at all. So the golden rule is, make sure the person serving you is an angler.

Then we have the part-time dealer. This is the shop which sells fishing tackle as a sideline. His main concern may be pet food, hardware, gardening equipment, fancy goods or toys. This does not mean to say that he is not a good tackle dealer. Fishing tackle is a seasonal trade and many people need to sell other things to keep their business going during the close season and winter months, when the demand for tackle and bait falls off. But some shops are tackle shop first and other goods second, whilst other shops are other goods first, tackle shop second. It is here that many pitfalls occur. Ask your friends, or people you know who are keen anglers, which shop they think is the best in the area, and if possible ask them to go with you.

The second thing a tackle dealer needs is time. Time to serve you and to advise you. Time to let you examine and set up rods and reels, though no tackle dealer has the time to do all these things on a Friday evening or a Saturday morning.

This is the period when every angler in the area will be coming into the shop for his weekend supply of bait and small items of replacement tackle. Many will be on their way home from work, or in for their weekend shopping. They will have cars parked on yellow lines or wives waiting on street corners with bags full of groceries. They want to be in and out in seconds and no tackle dealer can afford to spend half an hour advising you properly when he has a shop full of keyed up customers.

The best time to go into the shop is in mid-week, in the daytime if possible or late on Saturday afternoons, if weekends are the only time you can go. By then the rush will have died down and the dealer will have more time on his hands.

The third thing a tackle dealer needs is to know where you will be fishing. Will you be mostly fishing still water, or will you be on a river or perhaps both? Find out which waters in your area are available to you, if you can get day tickets, and most important of all, which waters contain catchable fish.

It is no good starting to learn fishing on a fast running deep river, or on a deep featureless lake with a large windswept area. Neither is it any good going to the local canal if it is badly polluted and has no decent head of fish in it. So ask around your friends who go fishing. Find out if they are prepared to show you around and explain what type of fishing you will be doing. Only then, when you are armed with this information, should you go to the tackle shop. Tell him your future plans, then he will have a good idea what rod will be the best and which range of floats you will need to fish these waters. Most important of all, what does he use on these waters, not just what he thinks you should use.

So we are now about to enter the world of the tackle shop. As we go through the door we notice thousands of different items around us. The counter festooned with different types of floats, weights, hooks and accessories. The walls lined with rods of all different lengths, thicknesses and colours. Nets and frames hanging from the ceilings, baskets, brollies, holdalls and bags. Where on earth do we start? How much must we buy? What do we really need to start with, and more importantly, what can we do WITHOUT?

2 RODS

Yes, the rod, the all important item. How do we choose from the hundreds that are available?

For general coarse fishing, most of the rods in the lower-to-mid price range of the more well known firms such as Shakespeare, can be relied upon for quality in design and performance, and give excellent value for money. These companies retain the services of top anglers in their various fields as consultants in the design and development of their equipment, thereby keeping in touch with the endless requirements of club and open match anglers, specimen hunters, and sea and game fishermen. The introduction of carbon fibre and other aerospace materials has in turn been reflected in the design of their rods, which are becoming lighter and more finely tuned instruments with each passing season.

The main points to consider when buying your first rod are where you are likely to do most of your fishing, and what methods and type of fish are to be considered. Also, your immediate ambitions must influence your choice, and of course the amount of money you are prepared to spend. If you intend to fish both flowing and still waters and also go on trips with a local club, then a 13' rod from the middle of the range upwards must be your first consideration. If you only intend fishing your local pond or canal on an occasional basis, then

Fig. 1. Modern Course Fishing Rods.

one of the budget float rods available from one of the large well known manufacturers will be more than adequate.

Always look for a rod of 12—13 feet in length with a nice firm action, made of hollow glass or carbon fibre. Avoid any rods which feel top heavy or sloppy. A good rod of this length will always have at least 10 rings on it. Avoid any rods that are sparsely ringed. The first rod you buy will have to perform numerous tasks. It must be able to cast a small float as well as a large float, it must have a sensitive response to small fish, but must also give you a chance to control and play the odd good fish that turns up when you least expect it.

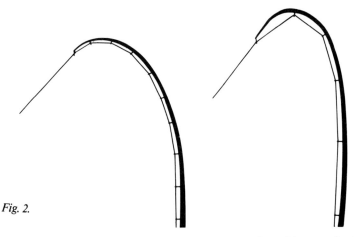

Fig. 2.

Rod with correct number of rings. The line will accurately follow the rod's curve.

A sparsely and incorrectly ringed rod. Excessive wear on both line and rings will result from this.

A good modern rod blank will never wear out if looked after properly. They do not kink or warp and the rod rings can always be replaced, so consider buying the best rod you can afford with regard to your ambitions and the variety of waters you intend to fish. As you progress in experience and ability you will be able to assess the individual merits and limitations of the various rods and develop a personal taste for a certain type of action, feel and design, with regard to the conditions you know you will face.

Until you have acquired this experience you will have to rely on the advice of your tackle dealer, which will be based upon the information you give him as to your future plans, and your own instinct as to whether the rod feels right for you. Remember a good rod is an extension of your right arm. Always, when buying a rod, assemble it and take it outside the shop to try it and get the feel of it. Ask your dealer to fit a reel to the rod or take your reel with you when you go to buy it. It can feel fine when trying it in the shop without a reel but be totally out of balance when you fit a reel to it and start fishing. The very 'top of the range' match rods are designed to be used with the latest top flight carbonite bodied reels, so this must be taken into account if you are investing into the top end of the market. A top quality rod fitted with a cheap die cast reel will not feel right, and neither will the reverse. Always buy rod and reel combinations from the same relative part of the range.

Many of the large tackle firms are now able to offer budget priced carbon rods for very little more than the cost of a glass-fibre rod. This does not mean that glass-fibre is now virtually obsolete as a rod building material. Some rods are now being designed, using a mixture of carbon and glass fibre sections built into their construction. This is because some of the qualities of glass fibre cannot be simulated with a 100% carbon fibre construction at a reasonable cost. This applies especially to match leger rods which are designed to be fished with fine hooklengths for large fish such as bream. Because these rods are placed on rodrests whilst fishing, as opposed to being hand held, the through action and shock absorbtion qualities of glass fibre more than makes up for the increased weight in the top and middle sections. A range of modern coarse fishing rods, including a top flight Boron rod, a budget carbon float rod, and a graphite and glass fibre mix swingtip rod, is shown in Fig. 1.

3 REELS

Reels come in all shapes, sizes, and types. In some respects choosing a good reel is more difficult than choosing a rod. You can see and feel the business side of a rod, but in a reel the works are inside the casing, and tackle dealers will not let customers loose with a screwdriver. So first of all we will look at the types of reel and which reels we do not want to buy.

The Centrepin

I love centrepin reels. I have half a dozen or so of different types, from a Match Ariel to a hand made ball bearing type. I always use a centrepin reel in preference to any other when the range and type of fishing allows, but inexperienced anglers should avoid centrepin reels, unless they have had a lot of practice, are efficient in tackle handling, and are prepared to pay £20 or more for one; centrepin reels should be forgotten at this stage.

Fixed Spool Reels

These are the reels you should be looking at. There are two basic types. The open spool type with bale arm pick-up and the closed face roller pick-up type. The open spool type with bale arm, is the most popular type and the largest range of reels falls into this category. They vary in price from a few pounds to over £40. There are hundreds to choose from, some are good, some are awful, some last for years. Others fall to bits on the first outing, chew the line up, or tangle the line round the back of the spool. But they all have one thing in common. The spools are too deep. Most of your fishing will be within 20 yards or less, so 100 yards of line is all you will need on your reel. The only trouble is that if you only put 100 yards of 2½ lb line on these spools, casting is an impossibility. So no matter which make of reel you buy, this next paragraph is the most important one in the book. If you do this correctly 90% of all the problems anglers have with casting and retrieving line will be solved.

When you buy a reel the first step is to select a ball of wool or string which is smooth. Tie this to the spool and wind on under slight tension until the spool is filled to within $^3/_{16}$" to ⅛" (4 mm) below the lip. Attach your 100 yard spool of line to the end of the wool, making sure that the knot lies tucked well down at the back of the spool, then wind the line on top of the wool. You now have a reel that will cast properly.

Back to buying that first reel. All reels take a lot of abuse. No matter how careful we are, reels get dropped. Rods fall off rests, reels fall in the mud or water, or onto stone canal towpaths. They get jammed with line or groundbait. They get trodden on whilst packing up, so it is important to buy a reel that has a good after-sales service behind it.

The more well known manufacturers like Shakespeare, carry this service.

The more obscure imported types do not. Ask your tackle dealer to show you the most popular makes of reels and ask if there is a service centre in this country.

Now let's look at the reels themselves. Avoid large cumbersome looking reels. These are unnecessarily heavy and awkward to use and are unsuited to the line strengths you are likely to be using. The bail arm should open and close smoothly. If you have to force the handle over hard to engage the pick up then avoid that reel. The line guide on the arm should be looked at closely. Some of the cheap reels with roller guides have gaps between the roller and the arm, into which the line can get trapped or damaged. Folding handle locking devices should also be looked at. Choose a reel with a screw locking system. Avoid those with spring clip devices; these tend to get clogged with mud, or the clip wears and does not hold properly, causing the handle to 'fold' when you reel in.

Fig. 3. Reliable reels with a full after sales service.

The slipping clutch is a very important part of a fixed spool reel. This device is to allow a fighting fish to take line if it suddenly lunges or bores away from you. It also helps to stop you breaking your line if you should strike too fiercely, a common occurrence with inexperienced anglers. Check that it operates smoothly at heavy as well as at light settings. If it feels jerky or sticky then avoid it. Do not accept the old sales line that 'it will free off with use'. Make sure that the Anti-Reverse lever works positively and can be operated without having to fumble for it. This device is to enable you to back-wind when playing a good fish, and is normally left in the 'on' position whilst fishing. Last but by no means least, check that the reel revolves smoothly without vibration. Try winding it at speed, and if you feel any wobble of the revolving head, avoid it. Always try to choose a reel from the middle of the range upwards. Cheaper models, though they may look the same, are made of lower quality materials. They have to be, to be cheaper, and they are not made to such close tolerances as the dearer models, so they have what is called inbuilt obsolescence. As with the rods, a couple of extra pounds spent on getting a good reel as opposed to a cheap one, can save pounds in the long term, also adding pleasure to your fishing that is beyond price.

A common mistake young and older newcomers to the sport make when buying or using a reel, is to use the wrong 'hand'. If you are right-handed, you use a left-hand wind. If you are left-handed, a right-hand wind. Otherwise you find yourself 'changing hands' when playing and reeling in fish. This is a very dodgy practice, and one that can lose you a lot of fish. It also makes your fishing awkward and clumsy instead of smooth and controlled.

Fig. 4. Correctly and incorrectly filled spools.

Most modern reels are designed to be ambidextrous, which means they can be used either right or left handed. But there are still some models that do not have this facility, and you need to state which hand you require when ordering or purchasing them.

Closed Face Reels

Though there is not such a varied range of these reels, more and more are being seen at the waterside. They do not have the casting range of the open type, but they are easy to operate and are ideal for trotting in flowing water. When you trap the line with your finger to strike, whilst using an open face reel with the bail arm open, it is difficult to engage the pickup to reel in the fish without slackening the line. With a closed face reel this is a straightforward and smooth operation. They are also an advantage when fishing in a strong wind, as there is no bail arm for the line to get blown around and tangled.

4 LINE AND HOOKS

Most anglers take their line and hooks for granted. In these days of mass production, anglers buy their line over the counter assuming that the spool being the same brand as the last spool they bought, is the same quality, breaking strain and diameter as all the others. This is a quite justified attitude to take and one that the line manufacturers encourage. Unfortunately this is not a perfect world. The line should leave the factory in first class condition, but modern inspection standards are not perfect. The odd bad batch does slip through unintentionally. Hook tempers also vary. The very nature of a hook being thin and delicate, does mean that heating and cooling temperature variations are quickly absorbed by the wire and faulty batches do get to the shops. Any angler worth his salt tests a line for brittleness and faults and a few hooks from a box of 50 for temper before accepting them and leaving the shop. If the tackle dealer objects, change your tackle dealer. Although I must stress that most good dealers worth their salt will probably admire any angler who shows he knows what he wants, and very few would object.

A lot happens to fishing line when it leaves the manufacturers. Most line is imported from Europe, so it has a good journey ahead of it before it reaches the distributors. Then it is probably hanging around in storage for a few months. Eventually it gets to the tackle dealer and then over the counter to you. During this period it is probably subject to an infinite number of variations in air temperature and humidity. Also in some cases uneducated dealers display it in the shop window for months on end, subjecting it to light variations. Avoid any spools of line where the label looks faded or dusty. Good tackle dealers leave the line in the box until a customer asks for it.

Ask your tackle dealer which brand of line he sells the most of, or keep your eyes and ears open and see what the other anglers are buying over a period of time. Try different popular brands until you find one that you can get on with. No two brands of line are the same. Don't buy cheap lines; buy lines in the middle price range. Cheap lines tend to be thicker in ratio to breaking strain than dearer lines and are stiffer, more brittle, or prone to kinking and twisting. As most anglers fish at close to medium range, a softish line with a bit of elasticity (stretch) is the most suitable. When you are inspecting a prospective purchase, unwind 12-18″ off the spool and pull gently to see that it 'gives' a bit. Hold it up to the window and see that it is even all the way along and that there are no light flecs in it showing up faults. If there are, avoid it.

Hooks come in so many shapes, types and sizes that a whole book would be needed to describe them all. So for simplicity I have made up a chart of suggested types for certain types of fishing.

Balance of line strength to hook type and size is also very important. For example; you would not tie a size 12 forged hook to a 1 lb B.S. hook length as the line strength is too fine to drive the hook home. Alternatively you wouldn't tie a size 20 hook to a 3 lb hook length. Even if you got a bite on it you would probably pull the hook out of the fishes lip whilst playing it. Also, the thick line would upset the delicate presentation you were trying to achieve by using a 20 hook in the first place, so it is doubtful if you would get many bites.

Let's have a look at a hook. It is classified by several different names, each one describing the various parts in its make up (see Fig. 5). It has a shank — this can be short, medium or long. It has a bend — this can be a crystal bend or a round bend. It then has a point — this can be straight, curved, beaked, or hollow ground. It can have a long point, a short point, a large barb or small barb, or no barb at all. Then we have the cross section of the wire. It can be fine wire, standard wire or it can be flatted and forged. All this is very confusing, so let's try and simplify things a bit.

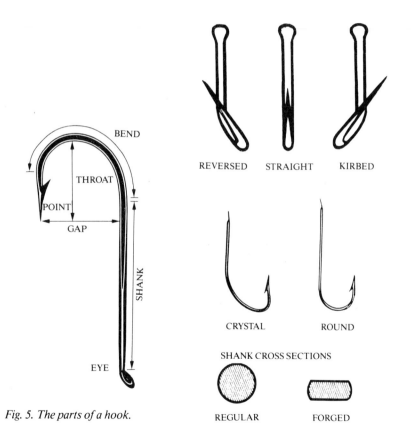

Fig. 5. The parts of a hook.

REVERSED   STRAIGHT   KIRBED

CRYSTAL   ROUND

SHANK CROSS SECTIONS

REGULAR   FORGED

For general float fishing with maggots, punched bread, hemp etc. for small to medium size fish, a standard or fine wire crystal bend hook with a medium shank size 14-22 is just the job. For fishing with casters where the hook needs to be buried completely in the bait or for fishing with a small worm, a fine wire round bend with a medium to long shank and hollow ground point is the hook to use. When fishing for large or powerful fish like tench, big perch, chub, barbel, bream and big roach, a forged hook size 6-16 is the type to go for. But the only way of ensuring you have the right type of hook to do the job, tied to the right strength of line, is to buy loose hooks and learn to tie your own.

Most inexperienced anglers rely on ready tied hooks in packets, where a hook is already whipped onto a length of line. Here lies the biggest pitfall for inexperienced anglers. For some reason known only to themselves, some tackle manufacturers still insist on using the obsolescent X grading for the hook lengths. This is a throw-back to the old days before nylon monofilament line when the hook length was made of cat gut. The thickness not the breaking strain was the governing factor. It was measured and given an X rating. I'm quite sure that even the tackle dealers have now forgotten what these ratings mean. So how on earth are we to know? I stopped using ready tied hooks 20 years ago and I assumed that some progress had been made in this department since then — but NO. Still anglers have to put up with fine hooks connected to ship's hawsers. Some of the better quality brands do, I know, have a reasonable degree of balance. But for some reason these are not finding their way into some angler's hook wallets. Learn to tie your own hooks and not only will you cut your hook bill down to a quarter of what it is now, but you will increase your catch rate considerably. Also if you get snagged on weed or other obstructions, you know you will break off at the hook length and not lose your float and yards of line. You can always be certain that the hook length is of a lower breaking strain than your mainline. The recommended hook length to mainline strengths are listed on the chart.

The best type of hook to buy for tying your own is the spade end in the sizes between 22-12. Eyed hooks in these smaller sizes tend to have too long a shank or too big an eye and make the hook unnecessarily heavy and awkward, especially when using small baits like maggots and casters. Also, they do not come in such a wide range of types. Eyed hooks are fine in the larger sizes. When you are using bread flake or paste baits, the eye is covered by the bait. Several good hook tyers are on the market now, but try to do the job by hand, then you won't be caught out if you should lose or forget to pack your hook tyer. Don't make too many hooks up at a time, as they will probably go rusty in their packets before you use them. When you first start trying to tie your own, practice on the bigger hooks first. You can see better what you are doing and can grip them better. As you get used to using your fingers, then you can attempt the smaller hooks.

Hook Type	Sizes	Breaking Strain Hook Length	Breaking Strain Main Line
Crystal Bend	22-20	1 lb-1½ lb	1½ lb-2½ lb
Crystal Bend	18-14	1½ lb-2½ lb	2½ lb-3 lb
Fine Wire Round Bend	18-14	1½ lb-2½ lb	2½ lb-3 lb
Forged	14-10	2½ lb-3½ lb	3½ lb-4 lb
Forged	8-6	Tied direct to main line	4 lb-6 lb
Forged	4-2	Tied direct to main line	6 lb-15 lb

Note the double line on the chart. Hook sizes 4-2 should not be used with lines of less than 6 lb and your float rods should not be used with a line in excess of 4 lb B.S. Special rods are needed with test curves of 1 lb plus to handle lines heavier than 4 lb. These are covered in later chapters. The average test curve of your float rods will be 10-12 ozs. Under certain match fishing situations, when it is necessary to use small 16 to 20 hooks for large fish such as bream, a forged pattern in these sizes must be used to prevent the hook from straightening out under the increased pressure.

Modern float and match leger rods allow you to use these small forged hooks on fine 1½ lb and 2½ lb hooklengths without risk of breakage in open snag free waters. Only experience will teach you just how much pressure you can use when playing large fish on this equipment. When fishing in areas with heavy weed or snags, the larger hooks with heavier lines must be used.

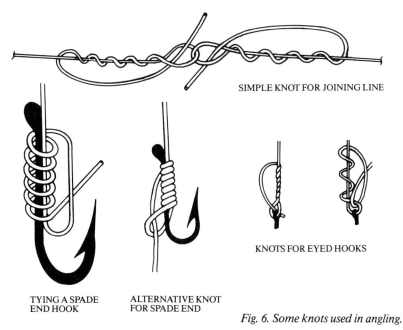

SIMPLE KNOT FOR JOINING LINE

KNOTS FOR EYED HOOKS

TYING A SPADE END HOOK

ALTERNATIVE KNOT FOR SPADE END

Fig. 6. Some knots used in angling.

13

5 OTHER EQUIPMENT

These are many and varied. No two tackle boxes you will see by the waterside contain the same number or types of items. Most anglers differ in their preference and use of equipment.

The items I describe in this chapter are all items you will need to fish effectively and correctly. Some are essential right from your first outing. Others can be added as and when you can afford them, or when you can no longer do without them as your ability and knowledge progresses.

Floats and legering tackle are dealt with in their respective chapters. The equipment I am about to describe are items that are used in conjunction with your rod and reel. As with these, there is a lot of rubbish on the market that you will need to avoid. There is also a lot that can be made by yourself, and these are dealt with in the chapter on tackle making.

The Hook Disgorger
The most important accessory you will need and one that you should never go fishing without, is one of the cheapest items in the tackle shop. This is the hook disgorger. This item is used to remove hooks from a fish's mouth or throat that cannot be reached by your fingers without causing the fish distress. It consists of a thin piece of aluminium or plastic rod with either a slotted barrel or a ring on the end. Avoid any so called hook disgorgers that are forked or V'd at the end. They do not work efficiently and the prongs rip into the fish's mouth or throat, causing severe damage to the tissue. The correct way to use the disgorger is to locate the line into the slot keeping the line taut. Slide the disgorger down the line until the hook shank is located into the barrel of the disgorger. Then with gentle downwards pressure the hook point is pushed out and lifted clear of the fish's mouth.

When using large or eyed hooks sizes 12 to 2's, a ring type, or better still artery forceps should be used. Always use gentle downwards pressure. Never twist or pull a hook from a fish. If the hook is right down the back of a fishes throat and cannot be seen or felt with the disgorger, do not poke around blindly. It is better to cut the line as far down the fishes throat as possible, leaving the hook in the fish. In most cases the fish will survive and get rid of the hook naturally.

To assist easy unhooking always use barbless or micro barb hooks, or squeeze the barb down on your hooks with a pair of pliers where possible. This will give your hooks better penetration and fewer fish will be lost or damaged by hooking.

The Landing Net
If you cannot afford a landing net when you first start fishing, always try to go

with someone that has got one, or fish near another angler who has a net. Any fish of 4 ozs or more should not be lifted from the water without the use of a landing net, otherwise the hook can rip out of the lip, or tissues in the throat will be damaged.

If you intend to buy a new landing net, try to get the largest you can afford and buy one of the knotless fine mesh types. The old type knotted nets with wide mesh are notorious for getting your terminal tackle tangled. With the fine mesh nets, your leger weight or shots cannot fall through the mesh and tangle. The knotless nets do not damage the fish's gills and fin spines, as used to be the case when they got trapped and tangled in the large mesh. Also the knots would lift and rub off the scales.

A telescopic handle is more versatile than a fixed handle. Not only does it give you more reach, but a weed cutter can be fixed in the end and the extra length reduces the distance you will need to wade out from the bank to clear an opening in a weedy swim.

Keep Nets

These are used when it is necessary to retain fish in a fishing match, or when the return of fish immediately to the swim will disturb your chances of catching any more. Never keep fish in a keep net unless it is really necessary.

Avoid any keep nets made of knotted mesh. Apart from the damage they cause to the fish, they are now illegal in many Water Authority areas. Buy knotless keepnets with a minnow size mesh. Micro mesh nets are also illegal in some areas. Make sure the length, mesh and ring diameter conforms to your local Water Authority regulations.

Check on your local regulations and if possible buy a net with the type of mesh I recommend, with a length of at least 8 ft and a ring diameter of at least 18 in. This size of net will be acceptable in any of the areas you may visit.

To secure the net to the bank you will need a bank stick. Do not buy a thin bank stick, they will not stick into the ground securely and they tend to spin or collapse; always buy a bank stick of at least 12 mm diameter. The standard thread on all angling accessories such as keepnets, landing nets and rod rest heads is ⅜ " B.S.F.

Rod Rests

Do not buy rod rests with thin wire or plastic forks and thin stems. Always buy the wide flat topped rod rest heads that screw into a bank stick (see Fig. 7). Avoid solid steel rod rests with rubber covered forks and bank sticks with tubular steel painted stems. As well as being heavy they also rust badly. Always buy bank sticks made from aluminium tube with brass threads. These will last a lifetime if looked after. Make sure that the tubing stretched across the top of the rod rest heads is made of plastic or polythene. Rubber gets hard and cracks or the metal rod breaks through at the edges. If you already have these and the rubber is wearing, don't throw them away. Polythene tubing can be bought for just a few pence from model shops or aquarists. Take your rod rest head with you so you get the correct bore of tubing.

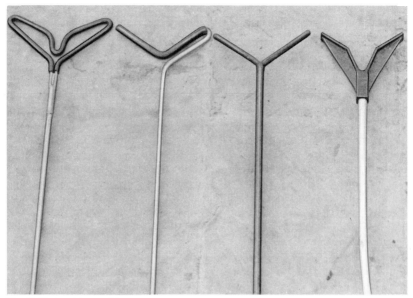

Fig. 7. Rodrests to avoid.

Tackle Boxes
The last couple of years has seen a fantastic improvement in the design and quality of tackle boxes. Up until then unless you made your own, which is still the best and cheapest way of acquiring a tackle box, you had to choose from a range of hideous and over priced American style cantilever boxes, made of brittle and easily broken plastic with narrow compartments into which nothing would fit. These boxes are O.K. if you fish American style for pike with plugs and spoons, but are useless for general coarse fishing. They have a habit of flying open when you least expect them to, scattering your tackle all over the bank. Or, if your basket falls over, all the bits and pieces of tackle you have spent hours separating into various compartments become one big tangled mass of loose bits and bobs in the bottom part of the box. Avoid cantilever tackle boxes.

A good tackle box is flat and has the compartments sensibly laid out in various lengths and widths, with the top of the tackle compartment fitting flush over the tray. It can be turned upside down or any other way when closed without the tackle moving about or getting mixed up. (See Fig. 8).

In my particular box, I have compartments for putting in loose shot so they are all easily got at without having to undo various boxes and tubs. Even the number 13 shots stay put when the box is fastened.

Some boxes like my own, also have a separate float compartment above the tackle compartment. These have slotted foam inside into which the floats are held separately, all in full view and easily selected. (See Fig. 9).

Bait Containers
These are made from plastic or polythene and are easily washed and cleaned. They can be of the flat round type or the bucket type with a wire carrying handle. They come in all sizes, some holding up to 2 gallons, but the 2 pint capacity containers are the most popular. A good bait bucket can be made from the plastic containers used on building sites or by handymen. These have been used to hold putty or tile adhesives or other building materials. Once the contents have been used they are normally thrown away. So, if there is any building work going on in your area ask the foreman if he can save you any used containers.

Margarine tubs also make good containers for seed baits like hemp, tares or sweetcorn, even maggots when only a few are needed. Make sure if you are using home made containers for live baits such as maggots or worms that you put plenty of air holes in the lid, but don't make them so big that the bait can climb out.

Tackle Carriers
These come in various types, from the traditional basket to the plastic and fibreglass boxes, or the framed type with waterproof covering. The function of a tackle carrier is twofold, firstly to provide an easily portable means of containing all the equipment needed at the bankside, and secondly to provide a seat for the angler to allow him to fish in comfort. Most of the types on the market have one thing in common; they are very expensive. A good tackle carrier can be made for less than a couple of pounds even if all the materials have to be purchased, leaving the newcomer more money to spend on buying a good rod or reel.

Umbrellas
A good angling umbrella is an essential item of equipment. As well as allowing you to fish in comfort in wet or windy conditions, it is also essential to prevent your tackle and bait from getting wet. Also, on hot summer days it provides shade for yourself and more importantly for your bait. Maggots soon stretch and die in hot weather if left in direct sunlight. Always fit guy ropes to the top of your umbrella and peg it down securely. They are too expensive to have them blown away into the middle of the river, which often happens when anglers don't tie them down properly. Always open them against the direction of the wind.

Rod Holdalls
These are essential items to have especially when your collection of rods, landing net handles, banksticks and umbrella uncreases. They allow all these items to be carried easily with less chance of breakage.

When buying a holdall, always buy one that will allow plenty of room for any future tackle such as roach poles and additional rods. The best holdalls I have found are the roll-up type or the tubular type that take the plastic tubes

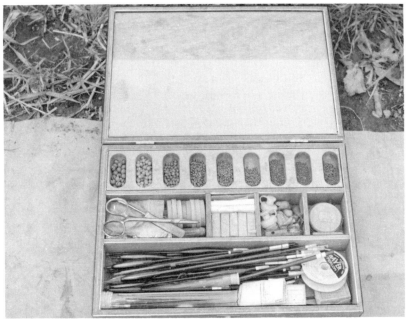

Fig. 8. Tackle box with individual shot compartments.

Fig. 9. A well laid out float box.

and have velcro fastenings. Avoid the narrow tubular holdalls with zip fasteners. The zips tend to get clogged up with mud and often break, and there is a strong chance of damaging your rod rings as you push or force your rods down inside. One big advantage of the roll up type is that all the items are laid side by side in their various compartments, and then rolled up when you have finished fishing. You can easily do a spot check to make sure you have packed everything and you can tell at a glance if anything is missing. Another big thing in their favour is that they are generally cheaper than the other type and more hardwearing, so they last longer. (See Fig. 10).

Catapults and Throwing Sticks
When fishing at a distance, or when the wind is strong, it is impossible to throw your loose feed out accurately without scattering it all over the place. In these circumstances a catapult or throwing stick is used. I prefer to use a throwing stick whenever the range I need to feed at allows. This is because a throwing stick can be filled and used with one hand. In other words, I do not have to put the rod down to feed. This is a big time saver when match fishing and when pleasure fishing if you need to feed during the period when you are trotting your float down stream.

When using a throwing stick you do not follow through with your arm. You have to bring it to a dead stop just in front of your head to eject the bait with enough force to make it go out to where you want it and to contain it in a nice tight formation. It is surprising just how far you can get your bait out, especially casters. As with a lot of things in angling, only practice makes

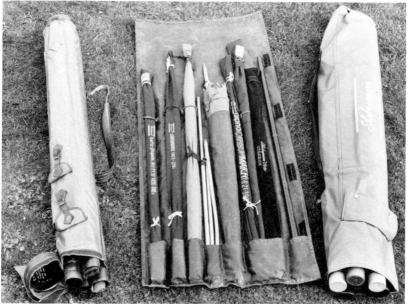

Fig. 10. Rod Holdalls.

perfect, but after a few outings when you have got the feel of it, greater accuracy can be obtained, and in a lot of cases far more easily than with a catapult or by hand throwing.

A good throwing stick can be made easily and cheaply from a bit of plastic tubing (see Fig. 104). I always cut the bottom of the throwing stick at an angle. This allows you to stick it in the bank in a verticle position so it can be loaded and picked up without even having to take your eyes off the float. One of a larger diameter can be made to throw small balls of groundbait, achieving greater distance and accuracy than when throwing by hand, and with less chance of the ball breaking up in mid-air as it often does when using a catapult.

When buying a catapult for long range feeding, always check with the dealer to be certain that he can supply spare elastics and pouches. Catapults are quite expensive items for what they are, and if your elastic breaks, which it can do quite frequently, you want to be able to repair it cheaply and not have to fork out for a new one.

The best type of pouches for loose feeding are the soft leather cone shaped pouches as opposed to the ones with the plastic cups. These keep your bait in a tighter formation than the cups, which tend to scatter the bait. Also they are less painful, especially on a cold day, when the cup flies over and cracks you on the knuckles. Always hold the catapult sideways when you fire it as opposed to vertically. This cuts down the chances of the cup flying round and hitting your knuckles. Believe me, when it does it is very painful!

The Bread Punch
I consider this to be an essential item of tackle, especially for fishing in still waters such as ponds, lakes and canals during the summer months. It is made of aluminium with a selection of brass heads that screw into the end and are stored inside the body when not in use. It allows you to put a tiny pellet of slightly compressed bread onto a small hook such as a size 16 or 18. This then swells up in the water covering the hook completely, making a nice soft, attractive bait. Always use medium or thick sliced bread as the thin sliced does not compress enough.

You lay the slice onto a hard surface such as a tackle box lid, and press the punch into the bread. This cuts the bread leaving a small pellet inside the head of the punch. You then insert the hook point, remove the pellet from the head, and gently position it around the bend of the hook. It is then ready to be cast in.

Always use fresh bread. Never take more than half a slice out of the bag at any one time or it will go dry before you have used it all. Used slices that have gone dry can be mashed up with water in a bait container, and small pieces can be flicked in around the float to attract fish into the swim.

In sunny conditions, try to keep all the bait in the shade so it will last you all day. This is one of the cheapest but most effective methods of fishing that there is.

6 BAITS

Almost any edible item can be used to catch fish, from soaked cornflakes and baked beans to swan mussel and big black slugs. Some baits produce almost instant reaction from the fish, others have to be introduced to the fish over a long period of time before any reaction is achieved.

This is because some baits, due to their shape, odour or movement, are easily recognised by the fish as being food. Others, which are tasteless, inert or bear no resemblance to anything a fish can associate with being food, need a lot of time and patience on the part of the angler before the fish respond to it.

In very heavily fished waters where there is a large head of fish, the fish sometimes associate the more commonly used baits with the disturbing effect of being caught. Time spent in introducing a new bait to these fish can be very rewarding, but generally we tend to stick to the tried and trusted baits that bring an immediate response from the fish no matter which water we visit. These I will cover in this chapter, but as your skill and confidence progress, do not be afraid to try something new, especially on waters that you know contain fish which are not very responsive to normal baits.

Bread Baits

Bread is by far the most versatile and the cheapest bait there is. It can be used naturally in the form of flake, punched pellets or crust, or it can be used in paste form mixed with an endless list of other ingredients such as cheese, sausage meat, petfoods and patés. Also it forms the basic ingredient of groundbait, the use of which I shall describe later on.

Bread flake is normally used when fishing for the larger species of fish such as tench, chub, bream and carp. It is also a good bait for sorting out the better quality of roach and rudd. It is normally fished on the larger sizes of hooks, from size 12 up to size 2.

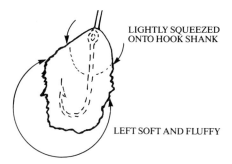

LIGHTLY SQUEEZED
ONTO HOOK SHANK

LEFT SOFT AND FLUFFY

Fig. 11. Putting bread flake on the hook.

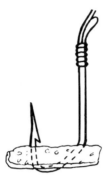 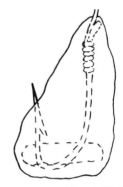

A PIECE OF CRUST IS FITTED ACROSS   PASTE THEN MOULDED AROUND
THE BEND OF THE HOOK   THE CRUST AND THE HOOK LEAVING
                                           THE POINT PROTRUDING

Fig. 12. Keeping soft paste on the hook.

A piece of bread is pulled from a fresh white loaf and gently squeezed onto hook shank, leaving the bread around the bend of the hook soft and fluffy (see Fig. 11). This makes a very attractive, slow sinking bait.

When the bait is to be fished using the smaller hooks, a bread punch as described in the chapter on angling equipment is the thing to use. This allows you to put a soft pellet of bread onto a fine hook without having to squeeze the bread onto the shank. The bait remains completely soft and fluffy at all times, and will swell up and cover the hook completely.

When you have finished fishing, always take any empty bread bags home with you. They are deadly to livestock if swallowed. If you start leaving litter on the bank you could very well lose your permission to fish.

When making bread paste, for use on its own or for mixing with other ingredients, dry bread must be used as opposed to fresh bread. It is soaked in water then placed in a lint free cloth and the excess water is then squeezed out until the paste is soft and sticky. If the additive is hard such as cheese, first grate it up fine before mixing in with the paste, kneading it until the bread and cheese are thoroughly mixed. It may take a bit of practice until the right consistency is obtained. Paste baits tend to harden in the water especially during cold weather, so always mix it as soft as possible but not so soft that it will not stay on the hook.

One way of keeping a soft paste on the hook when casting at long distances, particularly when freelining, when the bait is the only weight you have on the line for casting, is to use a piece of crust on the hook, onto which the paste is moulded. This also has the advantage of making the bait buoyant, which can be very important if fishing in a water with a soft mud or soft weedy bottom. The bait will lay on top of the mud or weed and not sink in, making it much easier for the fish to find (see Fig. 12). If using this method, always ensure that the hook point is well clear of the crust, otherwise the crust may cushion the point when you strike, preventing the fish from being hooked properly.

A very good paste additive for carp and tench is liver sausage paté. Every water I have tried this on which has contained carp and tench has responded immediately to it. It has a very strong odour and I normally mix it to the paste in a 50-50 ratio. It makes a very soft paste and I always use a crust on the hook to mould the bait onto.

You can experiment with different meat based additives and be confident that they will catch fish. If you fish a water with one additive and have a lot of success with it and then for some reason the fish stop responding, try a change of additive. Fish do become wary of certain baits after a time, and a change of bait can be sufficient to get the fish responding again.

Maggot Baits

Although bread is by far the cheapest bait, maggots are the most popular. Almost every angler you see fishing will have a container of maggots at the side of him. A lot of anglers would not even bother going fishing if they could not get their weekly supply, so preoccupied are they by this bait.

Maggots are a good bait. Because they are used so much the fish have come to accept them as a natural food. But even maggots have their off days and it's on these days that the more versatile angler can, by using something different, be the only person on the water who is catching fish. So do not become too preoccupied with maggots as bait.

Maggots are the larva of the fly. They are produced commercially. The flies are given the most ideal breeding conditions and the larva are provided with all the food they need to reach maximum growth in the shortest possible time.

The better the quality of the feed the better the quality of the maggot. As with all aspects of fishing equipment, the quality can vary from shop to shop.

In the case of maggots not only can the quality vary, but the quantity can as well. A good tackle shop sells you your measure of maggots neat. In other words the measure is of all maggots and the bran or sawdust is then added afterwards. Avoid tackle shops that do not bother to separate the maggots from the sawdust they arrive in from the bait farm. If they serve you with a measure of maggots mixed with dirty sawdust, not only are they giving you short measure, but they are also showing their total lack of interest in their customers' requirements.

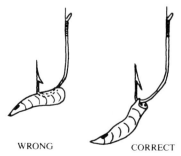

WRONG   CORRECT   THE CORRECT WAY
                                                    TO HOOK A CASTER

Fig. 13. Hooking a maggot.

23

Fortunately most tackle dealers are now better educated in the sale and presentation of their bait than they used to be, but always be on the lookout and avoid any bad dealers. Ask your friends or local match anglers which shops in your area are the best shops for supplying top quality bait. Match anglers in particular have to have the best quality of bait available in their area to be successful. So these are the best people to ask.

Commercial hook maggots are the larva of the Bluebottle fly. They can be bought in their natural colour which is white or they can be bought ready dyed in different colours. The most popular being yellow, and chrysodine which is a bronze colour. One important word about chrysodine dyes. Tests are revealing a connection between chrysodine dye and some forms of cancer. Good chrysodine substitute dyes are now becoming available, and these should be used in preference to actual chrysodine.

The popular belief is that fish are colour blind. This may or may not be so. It has yet to be proven one way or the other. Even so, fish do show a marked preference at certain times for one colour over another. This can vary quite frequently. One day they will go mad for a bronze maggot and ignore yellow or white, the next day only the white bait will catch fish. Why this is we do not know. What we do know is it pays to experiment with different colours at any one sitting just to find out what colour the fish are 'ON' that particular day.

When you go to your tackle shop for your bait, ask the dealer to give you a mixture of each colour. Most dealers now sell the bait already separated into their different colours, so if you ask for a measure of mixed colours he will give you some from each batch. Some dealers do mix their colours or buy ready mixed colours from the bait farm in which case they will be already in one container.

Always check your bait before you leave the shop to see that it is fresh and you have been given the type of bait you have asked for. A fresh maggot has got a black feed streak in the head. The more pronounced the streak the fresher the maggot is. If a maggot has not got a black streak then it is old and about to turn into a chrysalis. Do not be afraid to refuse old bait.

In the summer months, if you buy your bait on a Wednesday or a Thursday then the maggots will be minus the feed mark due to the high activity of the bait in warm conditions. But when you buy your bait on a Friday or at the weekend, the bait should be fresh as most tackle dealers take delivery of their fresh bait on a Thursday or Friday. If you are offered old bait on these days then you are within your rights to refuse it.

Always keep a bag of fresh bran or maize meal at home to clean your bait with. If the sawdust or bran in your maggots starts to turn dark, riddle it off and put your bait into some fresh stuff. Never leave the lid on your bait tin except when you are carrying it, especially in hot weather. This causes the maggots to sweat. When maggots sweat they start to climb or suffocate. The safest way to store maggots is with the lids off.

Pinkies

The maggot that is the most prone to climbing at the slightest hint of dampness is the 'PINKIE'. This is the larva of the Greenbottle fly. They are much smaller than the ordinary maggot or hook maggot as we call them. Pinkies are called 'feeder' maggots. They are used to feed a swim without over-feeding the fish, as can sometimes happen if you just feed hook maggots. The theory is that if you feed with pinkies the fish will then see the larger hook maggot you are using as your hook bait, and be overcome with greed to get at a larger tastier sample.

On a lot of occasions this method works, but on many others it doesn't. If you are feeding pinkies and fishing a large maggot on the hook, especially when the fish are mainly on the small side, they will become preoccupied with the smaller maggots and ignore the larger ones, or just suck the larger one at the end. In these circumstances it pays to scale down your hook size to a 20 or 22, and fish with a pinkie as your hook bait. In adverse conditions when the fish are not biting very freely, using the pinkie as a hook bait can get you the extra bites. I never go fishing without a supply of pinkies, especially if I am in a match. In fact I use more pinkies in the winter months than any other maggots.

Squatts

These are the larva of the common housefly. They are a very frail maggot and take a lot of keeping. You cannot fridge squatts like you can pinkies and hook maggots. They are very light in weight and it is here that their attraction lies. They sink very slowly and due to their softness and relatively inert state they can be mixed easily with the groundbait. They are mostly used by match anglers when swing tipping for bream. Several balls of groundbait and squatts are thrown into the swim. As the groundbait breaks up a very slow sinking cloud of food is produced, a cloud that is very attractive to the bream and it induces them to start feeding. You then cast your hook bait into the baited area and if the bream are feeding they have no difficulty finding your large hook bait in a cloud of tiny squatts.

On days when the fish are not feeding very well, a single squatt or a couple of squatts on a small hook can produce a few bites, but they do not keep very well and you should not bother buying squatts unless you are intending to fish for bream. Pinkies are a much better bet for a general alternative hook bait to the commercial hook maggot. Also, pinkies keep for longer than any other maggot before turning into a chrysalis. If kept cool in a fridge pinkies can last several weeks and still be good enough to use.

When fishing with maggots, always lightly hook the bait through the skin at the thick end of the maggot, taking care not to burst it, (see Fig. 13).

Casters

There are times when you want your hook maggots to turn into chrysalides. This is when you wish to produce casters. The caster is a very good bait and will catch all species of fish. Generally it will sort out the better quality fish from the small ones. Big roach especially like casters, as do perch, chub, bream and carp. But these fish only like good fresh casters, not stale, sour ones.

What then is a caster? Or more to the point, what is a good caster?

A caster is a maggot chrysalis in its very first stage of development. When a maggot first changes into a chrysalis it slows down its movements and starts to contract. Its skin then goes through a very rapid series of colour changes. A white maggot would begin to turn to a light yellow, to dark red, then to an almost black colour. At the same time as these colour changes are going on the metabolism of the maggot is also changing. One of the side effects of this changing process is the effect upon the buoyancy of the chrysalis. If allowed to go too far it will float. It is very important that the chrysalis is caught at the right stage of the changing process and the process slowed down, so that when you come to use the bait it will still sink.

The only way you can slow down the process is to reduce the temperature and the amount of air. The point at which you do this is between when the chrysalis is a light yellow and a dark orange in colour. If the chrysalis is allowed to get to the dark red stage then you will be too late as the bait will then float.

There are several ways of separating the bait at this point: one is to pick the casters off by hand as they turn at intervals of a couple of hours, or if a large quantity is required, to run the maggots through a 3 mm mesh. The live maggots will wriggle through the mesh leaving the casters and any dead maggots on the top of the riddle.

It is very important to remove any dead maggots from the casters at this stage as they rapidly decompose and will sour the bait if left.

The casters are then put into a plastic bag and stored in a cool place preferably in a fridge. If you store them in a fridge, do not put them in the freezer compartment as this will kill them. Although they are no longer wriggling they are still very much alive. Also, do not keep them in the bag for more than a day without opening the bag to allow some more air into it.

You want to reduce the amount of air they receive, not completely starve them of it. Never keep casters in water, this is the biggest cause of sour casters. They will just drown and start to decompose inside their shells. When you are actually fishing with them, especially in the summer, then you can put some water in the bait tin to stop them turning as they will be used straight away.

Casters should always be used within a couple of days from when they started to turn. Sometimes when turning our own casters they may start to turn on the Wednesday as you will be using them on the Sunday. In this case you must not keep them all this time in a plastic bag, otherwise they will die and turn black. What you can do is to keep them in a bait tin with the air holes covered up with cling film. This is the thin plastic wrapping film used in the kitchen.

After the first couple of days when you have turned say ¾ pint of casters, you take them out of the plastic bag and put them in a small 1 pint capacity bait tin, or margarine tub. You then put cling film over the top of the container and fit on the lid. This will stop any air getting into the container but at the same time leave a bit of air inside the container to keep the casters alive. You then store the container in a cool place or a fridge. In this way they will keep for up to 4-5 days.

When you buy your casters from the tackle shop they will be supplied in plastic bags and should be fresh. Certainly they should not be more than a day old. When you get them home, you should put them in a bait container and fit over the cling film. In this way they will keep much fresher than if they are left in the plastic bags. Avoid any shop bought casters that look 'burnt' where the casters are touching the side of the bag. This means they are several days old and are probably dead. Never buy casters that have been kept in water. A lot of dealers still keep their casters this way due to ignorance of the fact that casters die in water. Never subject your maggots to a lot of heat if you want good casters. Always keep them in a cool place and allow them to turn naturally. Forced casters are small and shrivelled looking and are no good at all.

In the winter you may have to bring them into the house to get them to turn in time for when you want them, but always leave them in the coolest place possible.

When fishing with casters, the hook is buried inside the caster. (See Fig. 13). If you are getting bites and the caster is being nipped off at the end and you are not connecting with the fish, then you can try fixing the caster onto the hook the same way as you would hook a maggot. A fine wire round bend hook with a medium to long shank is the best type of hook to use. If you ask your dealer for caster hooks he should know the type you want.

Hemp and Tares

A lot of nonsense has been talked and written about hempseed, some of which you may have heard about. One school of thought says that it drugs fish. This is not true. Also I believe it is false that fish, particularly roach, become preoccupied with it and will not feed on any other bait. What happens, I think, is that anglers abuse the use of it and the fish are so full of hemp that they are not inclined to feed on anything for a long time, that includes more hemp. Unlike maggots, hemp and tares are a solid bait. Maggots contain 90% water, whereas seed baits contain 90% of solid stodge which takes a fair time to pass through the fishes digestive system.

Seed baits should be used very sparingly. Senior and Junior anglers are guilty of over feeding, especially where seed baits are concerned. A dozen grains of hemp every couple of minutes are all that is required, not 3 or 4 handfulls.

Also most anglers prepare far more hemp and tares than they will ever need for a days fishing. Then at the end of the day with a pint or two of the stuff left over, they empty the contents into the water and then they wonder why the fish have 'gone off' the feed.

Never empty unwanted bait, especially unwanted seed baits into the water. Either take it home or throw it up the bank for the birds.

Tares or pigeon peas, are a brown dried type of pea with a shiny skin; both baits can be bought from seed merchants and pet shops.

To prepare them you need to soak them in water for at least 24 hours. This allows them to swell up slowly. In the case of tares, you do not want the skin to crack or burst when you cook them, so pre-soaking is essential. After pre-soaking you put them in a saucepan with plenty of water and a pinch or two of bi-carbonate of soda to bring out the colouring. This helps to make the hempseed go a nice black colour and the tares a rich brown.

THE HOOK IS PUSHED INTO
THE SPLIT OF THE HEMPSEED

TARES ARE HOOKED
JUST UNDER THE SKIN

Fig. 14. Hooking hemp and tares correctly.

You bring the saucepan up to the boil then turn the light down to low, to simmer the bait until it's ready. The hemp will be ready when the skin starts to split and the white kernel begins to show. The tares need to be soft so that they squash when you squeeze them. If they just split in two they are too hard and need further cooking. As soon as they are soft they are ready. Do not over cook them. Check them every minute or so, then remove them if the skins show any sign of splitting. Although the preparation of the two baits is the same they do take a different length of time to cook, so always prepare hemp and tares separately.

When using hempseed a size 16-18 hook is used. The seed is fixed to the hook by inserting the bend of the hook into the split (see Fig. 14). Sometimes, when the fish are feeding well, they will take your split shot in mistake for the bait. To avoid this you use a coil of fine gauge wire in place of the indicating shot or you can use celery shot or mouse droppings. This is the name given to the continental shot which is elongated as opposed to round.

For tares you use a size 16 or 14 fine wire hook. These are hooked just beneath the skin and stay on the hook much better than hempseed. Plenty of time must be given to allow the fish to take the bait. Unlike hempseed, which normally produces very fast bites, the fish take their time with tares and may bob your float for quite a long time before moving off with the bait. The bites, when they do come are normally a slow, steady disappearance of the float after the preliminary signals and are generally unmissable.

A ½ pint of hemp or tares is more than enough for a days fishing. A handful of dried tares will swell up to 2-3 times its volume when cooked.

Luncheon Meat

This has become a very popular and effective bait for chub and barbel but it has left in its wake a very disturbing side effect. Empty tins are being left on the bank or in the margins of the river. Farmers have been reporting serious foot injuries to their livestock and in some cases this has led to anglers being banned and fishing rights taken away. The best way to prevent tins being left at the waterside is not to take them there in the first place. Open your luncheon meat at home and cut or break it up before you go fishing. It keeps very well in an empty margarine tub or a bait tin with cling film under the lid.

It is normally fished legered on a size 8 to a size 4 hook depending on the size of fish you are after. It is better cut into thick slices and then break hook sized pieces off, rather than to cut it up into uniform cubes which could arouse suspicion from a prospective fish. Sometimes it is best mixed with soft bread paste as it tends to harden, especially in cold conditions, and could prevent the hook point driving home on the strike. Always make sure the hook point is clear of the bait to minimise the risk of missed bites.

Sweetcorn

This has been found to be a very effective bait after an extensive pre-baiting period, particularly for carp and tench. It is not an instant bait like bread or maggots. If you use it on a water where it has never been used before it will be necessary to pre-bait with sweetcorn over a period of days or even weeks until it is accepted by the fish. It can be fished singly on a size 14 or 12 hook, or in multiples if larger hooks are needed. As with luncheon meat, tins are becoming a problem, so prepare the bait at home.

Worms

Worms have been used as bait since angling first began in prehistoric times, but its amazing how many anglers do not know the correct way of putting a worm on the hook.

Much of a worms attraction to the fish is in its wriggle. Why then do anglers do their best to prevent the bait from carrying out this most important of functions? By looping it round and hooking it several times they prevent it wriggling. By hooking it through the saddle where all the essential organs of the worm are stored it will quickly die and stop wriggling. So how do you get the best from your worm?

A worm should always be hooked through the head. The hook point should be inserted just below the tip and come out again just above the saddle (see Fig. 15).

If hooked in this way it can wriggle freely and will last in the water for quite a considerable time. The main reason people fasten a hook through a worm several times is to stop the bait flying off the hook when they cast, but by doing this they are preventing the worm from doing its job as an attractor. If you are fishing at a long distance, the worm can be kept securely on the hook with either a caster or a maggot being put onto the hook after fixing on the worm. In the case of a large hook, a piece of bread flake or crust can be pressed onto the point to hold the worm on the cast and if not required it can be 'struck off' once the bait has landed in the water.

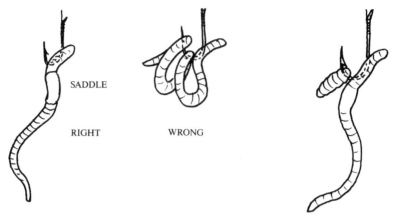

SADDLE

RIGHT   WRONG

Fig. 15. Hooking a worm.

WORM LOCKED ONTO THE
HOOK WITH A CASTER

Worms come in two sizes. The small red worm and brandling worms and the mighty lob worm.

The red worms and brandlings are ideal for general fishing for bream, tench, small perch and roach. The lob worms are used for chub, barbel, perch and carp.

Red worms and brandlings are fished on hooks from size 16 to 10. The lob worms from sizes 8-2's. They can be float fished, legered, or freelined, a very versatile bait. They can be fished singly or in bunches, or you can use just the head or tail.

Locating worms is also fairly easy providing there are no drought conditions prevailing.

Red worms or brandlings can be found underneath compost heaps or manure heaps. Lob worms are found in either the soil or on the surface of lawns at night. The worms found on the lawns are normally the biggest and the juiciest. Any mown grass area will have worms. Parks, garden lawns or grass verges on estates will have some, but some areas will be better than others. When you first go worm hunting it may take some time to find the most prolific areas. Once these are found only a few minutes work will be needed to replenish your stock.

The way to get them is to go out after dark when the grass is damp or wet with dew. Take a flash lamp with a shaded beam and a bucket to a probable area. Tread gently as any vibration will cause the worms to shoot back down their holes. The worms will be lying half in, half out of their holes, stretched out on top of the grass. When you pick one up in your torch beam its no good trying to grab it in your fingers as it will just contract and shoot down its hole. Look for the darkest part which is the head, then press hard down with your finger on the lightest end away from the head. The worm will contract, but will not be able to get past your finger. You then take hold of its head and gently ease it out of its hole. Do not pull hard or you will end up with only half of a worm which will quickly die.

Keeping worms can be difficult, particularly lob worms. These are very difficult to keep alive especially in bait tins. To keep lob worms in good condition for any length of time you must have a fairly large container such as a bath or large bowl placed in a cool shady place and half filled with good quality soil with several inches of grass cuttings on the top. This must be kept well watered but not too wet.

Keeping red worms or brandlings is a lot easier. Damp peat in a bait container is all that is needed, but if you want to toughen them up, damp moss is the best thing to use. By turning the tin over each day the worms will keep working down through the moss. This will produce very tough muscular worms with plenty of wriggle. Don't allow the peat or moss to dry out and make sure the air holes are clear.

Other Baits

Almost anything edible can be used as bait and some fish are caught on really strange concoctions. I once saw a ½ lb roach that was caught on a blackberry. Stewed wheat and barley can also be a very good particle bait, but it must be well soaked before being stewed. Be very careful not to use dried or dehydrated baits before soaking them first. Fishes digestive systems are not as advanced as ours and they cannot dissolve hard baits. There was a case not so long ago where anglers were using dried beans as baits without soaking them first. The carp ate lots of them and could not digest them. They just lay in the carp's stomachs until they started to swell up, bursting the fishes stomachs and killing them.

Elderberries when ripe can also be a good bait for roach. During a period of a few years ago when we couldn't get any maggots, my uncle took over 10 lbs of good roach on elderberries. I had a few maggots and all I could catch was gudgeon.

Another bait that used to work well on a stretch of water below a Canning factory was cooked peas. The fish were used to finding peas that were discharged from the factories outfall. So in that stretch of water they became a 'natural' bait.

I caught a good bag of trout in the upper Wharfe one spring using large nymphs I found in the water. I had fished all day with maggots and worms with very little to show for it, then whilst sitting on a rock waiting for his turn to fish this particular pool my companion noticed this large ugly looking nymph in the water. I put it on the hook just for a laugh, but it had not gone a few feet down the swim before the rod was nearly wrenched from my hand by a taking trout. We hurriedly turned over the rocks at the waters edge and collected a dozen or so of these beasties. We then went on to take a superb bag of trout and grayling.

Lob worms and minnows are noted chub baits, as are big black slugs and crayfish. A friend of mine who is a well known big fish man, once demonstrated the immense attraction of these on the River Wensum. He netted a dozen or so crayfish from a very clear lake near Norwich and kept them overnight in a bucket. The following day we went to a stretch on the Wensum that held a lot of big chub, but no crayfish. On his very first cast he hooked and landed a chub over 4 lbs and went on to take 8 fish in less than an hour from this stretch. This was an occasion that has impressed itself on my memory ever since. Tench and carp can be caught using swan-mussel or snails. Roach love caddis grubs, these are a truly natural bait like those funny nymphs we found and fish will take them with great confidence. Always match your hook size to the size of the bait you are using. Don't be frightened of using a large hook when it is necessary. It's no good using a small hook with a large bait, just as it is no use using a small bait with a large hook. Also make sure you balance the hook size to the correct line strength. Use the chart shown in the chapter on Line and Hooks.

Groundbait

Groundbait has two separate functions. The first is to provide an attraction to the fish and to hold them in a particular area of the swim, and the second function is to enable you to throw light samples of bait a long distance, containing it until it hits the water.

Normally both these functions go hand in hand, one being the means of achieving the other, but there are times when the use of groundbait can put an end to any chances of you catching fish.

In heavily fished waters the fish associate the introduction of groundbait with the unpleasant memory of being caught. As more and more people are coming into the sport, popular match venues are under increased pressure. The River Witham at one time was described as a river of groundbait with some water flowing over it.

The fish can get sick of the stuff, especially in still waters where the groundbait just lies on the bottom going sour after a period of time if the water does not hold a big enough head of fish to consume it all.

If used sparingly and carefully however, groundbait helps us to catch fish, but always loose feed whenever possible. If you think you can increase your catch by using groundbait, just mix a small amount to start with. Throw in a couple of tiny balls no bigger than the size of a walnut. If your bites increase then throw in a small soft ball every few minutes. But if the bites stop, it's no good throwing in any more. The thing to do is stop feeding groundbait and revert to just loose feed. Also, cut down on this as well. Throw in too much and you will over feed the fish. The reason your bites have stopped is because either the fish have moved away or they have stopped feeding. If there are no fish there, then your feed will just sink to the bottom, gradually piling up. When the fish return they will have to go through a lot of food before they find your bait, and by the time they have found it they may be too full to want any more.

Always think before you throw. Don't get into the habit of feeding just for the sake of it. Different waters require different approaches. Also, the approach to one water can alter from day to day as the conditions alter.

Most groundbait is made from bread. You can make your own groundbait quite cheaply just by saving any stale bread. When you have a reasonable amount, you bake it until it is brown, then grind it up in a mincing machine or liquidiser. I prepare all my own groundbait in this way. The secret is to dry the stale bread right out before you store it or bake it. If you do not do this, it will go mouldy when you store it and soggy if you try to bake it. I let mine dry hard by placing it on top of the central heating boiler, then, when it has dried out, I put it in a paper sack in a cupboard until I have collected enough to justify a groundbait making session.

Other ingredients can be added to the basic breadcrumb to make it perform as you want it to. In flowing water, clay or molehill soil can be added to make it sink faster. If a heavy mix is needed, bread soaked overnight in a bowl of water can be added after being squeezed out first. This heavy mix is only used when fishing for big fish and pre-baiting is an effective means of catching them in that particular water. When general fishing, just plain groundbait mixed with water to the right consistency is used. Groundbait should be *added to the water* until it is nice and fluffy. It should hold together when squeezed and thrown, then break up as it falls through the water.

Heavy balls that just fall to the bottom without breaking up are a waste of time and groundbait. So also is groundbait that has not been mixed with enough water. This will just float on the surface. Groundbait that does not hold together whilst being thrown is also useless. The ball will just split up in mid-air and scatter all over the place. Don't forget the object of groundbaiting is to concentrate the fish, not to scatter them. If extreme range is needed and you cannot throw that far, use a throwing stick or a catapult.

Do not expect to achieve all these things overnight. Accuracy and mixing are acquired arts. You will make a lot of mistakes before you get it right, so do not be too worried if you don't get it right first time.

Samples of the hook bait can also be mixed with the groundbait. Inert hookbaits such as casters, seedbaits and luncheon meat can be mixed in fairly large quantities, whereas maggots and pinkies can only be added sparingly, as the wriggle of the bait causes the ball of groundbait to break up too quickly, normally resulting in the groundbait splitting up in mid-air. The exception to this is when using squatts. Being relatively inert, small and soft, a large quantity can be mixed with the groundbait with little hindrance to the bait's throwing capabilities. In fact ground baiting is the only way of introducing squatts into a swim at any sort of range when fishing, as they are too light to be catapulted.

On waters where groundbaiting can have an adverse effect on the fish, always try to achieve the range by loose feeding with a catapult, or by using a blockend swimfeeder when legering, using groundbait as a last resort. In very windy conditions loose feeding with a catapult may not be easily or accurately achieved. In these circumstances, groundbaiting will have to be used. You would bait up with two or three balls of groundbait with your hook bait samples or feeders mixed in with them, and then leave the swim to develop. At no time would you throw in any more feed. This would only unsettle any fish that might be tempted to investigate the initial bait. Patience really is a virtue under these conditions. If fishing on a water where the fish respond to groundbaiting, you would still feed with a couple of balls to start with. If bites do not develop then it is pointless putting anymore feed into the swim. But if bites are forthcoming, an additional ball at regular intervals may keep the fish feeding, but do not overdo it. If the bites cease, then so should the groundbaiting. This will allow the fish to settle down again and hopefully start to feed once more.

7 THE FISH

To be successful, an angler needs to know about the various species of fish that are to be found in his local waters.

He needs to be able to identify them and know something about their habits and diet. If an angler wishes to catch a particular species then he must find the type of water that is suited to them and use a bait that will be accepted by the fish. He must fish this bait in such a way that the fish will take it naturally and without suspicion. To do this, the angler needs to know whereabouts in the water the fish feeds. Is it a bottom feeder, a midwater feeder or a surface feeder? Some fish, like the roach will feed at various levels, others like the tench and barbel are mainly bottom feeders, and it is there that the bait must be presented if these species are to be caught.

Very experienced anglers can tell just by the type of bite indication and by the way the fish fights, what species of fish they have hooked, without actually seeing the fish until it comes to the surface.

A quick glance is all that is needed to identify most of the various types of fish, due to obvious features such as their shape and colouring. Others, especially when they are small and of a similar size, can only be identified by careful examination of their fins or mouths. In the case of hybrids, which are cross breeds caused by different species spawning together in the same areas at the same time, laboratory examinations of their throat teeth and scale formations are sometimes necessary before true identification can be pronounced. This is now standard practice when rod caught records for similar species such as roach and rudd are being considered.

Before we go on to describe the individual species, let us first have a look at the external features of our quarry.

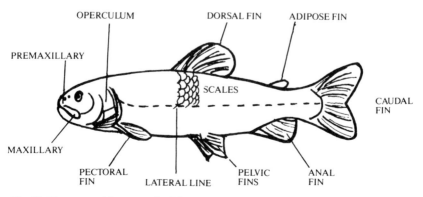

Fig. 15. The external features of a fish.

All the fins shown are standard on all coarse fish apart from the adipose fin which is only found on game fish such as trout, salmon and grayling. The grayling is a member of the salmon family of fishes but is classed as a coarse fish in many parts of the country. It is a very popular fish with those coarse anglers fortunate enough to have grayling in their local waters, but they are treated as vermin by the purist game anglers and river keepers, as are all coarse fish.

Exceptions to the rule are the perch, ruffe and zander. These have two full dorsal fins, the forward one being very hard and spiney, the rear one is soft. Care should be taken when handling these fish as they tend to hold their fins erect when they are frightened, and a badly cut hand can be the reward for carelessness.

The lateral line is another prominent feature on the fishes body. This line is a series of dashes running along the flank of the fish from the gill cover to the tail. The function of this line is to detect vibrations caused by other fishes movements or any bankside disturbance. Sound waves are transmitted through the water very quickly and a heavy footfall on the ground will be detected very easily by the fish. Sound waves through the air are not transmitted through the water quite so easily, so the noise from a bite alarm or from one angler talking to another will have very little detrimental effect. One of my favourite swims on the river Lark in Cambridgeshire, was directly under the flight path of R.A.F. Mildenhall, an American base into which the big Boeing super tankers used to land and take off. The noise from these aircraft was tremendous but it did not seem to worry the fish unduly.

One day I was catching lots of small roach and bream and several aircraft had landed and taken off without any slowing of the bite rate. Then several youngsters came running along the bank behind me coming to a halt with a jumping action just to the rear of where I sat. I never had another bite for the rest of the morning.

Scale counts along this line or vertical scale counts between the line and the dorsal fin, can be very useful for distinguishing similar species of fish, such as roach and rudd. On the roach there are eight scales between the dorsal fin and the lateral line, whereas the rudd has seven. As you can see, when you describe fish and their respective differences it is essential to know the names of the different fins and whereabouts on the fish these are located. Remember these and it will help when you need to enquire about any aspects to do with the fish, or have to describe and express yourselves to other anglers. We will now have a look at the fish themselves.

The Roach

The roach is the most widespread and due to this, the most popular of our coarse fish. It is a shoal fish and will feed at all levels in the water, but is mainly a bottom and midwater feeder. It prefers the slower reaches of the river to the faster flowing water, and is present in most still water fisheries from ponds to reservoirs. It will take a wide variety of baits. Maggots, casters, seed baits, bread and worms will all be acceptable to the roach, with bread flake being the better bait for tempting the larger fish.

The fish is silvery in colour with a bluish tinge across the flanks and a green or brownish coloured back. The fins vary from a pale orange to red in colour.

The Rudd

The rudd is mainly a surface and midwater feeder, prefering still waters to rivers. Again the rudd is a shoal fish. It is very similar to the roach in both shape and appearance, the main distinguishing features being the colouring, the shape of the mouth and the relationship of the dorsal fin to the pelvic fins.

Rudd again are basically a silver fish but have a golden or burnished tinge and the fins are a deeper red in colour, although these colours can vary from water to water. The rudd, being a surface feeder, has an upturned mouth and a slightly longer lower jaw. The roach has jaws of equal length giving it a straighter-mouthed appearance.

The leading edge of the dorsal fin starts behind a vertical line of the pelvic fin on the rudd, whereas on the roach the dorsal fin is positioned directly above the pelvics.

Due to their very close relationship and similar spawning habits, roach-rudd hybrids are very common in some waters. Rudd will take most of the baits recommended for roach but are not very bothered about seed baits. Bread, worms and maggots are the best baits for rudd.

The Bream

Bream are found in mainly slow moving and still waters, and are also closely related to the roach, but in the case of the bronze or common bream, these are easily distinguishable. They are a much more heavily built fish, with deeper rounder shape. The colour can vary from a pale bronze to an almost black colour in the older larger fish. The skimmer bream is a much smaller fish than its big brother and these can be distinguished from the roach by their deeper shape and long extended anal fin. Again due to its spawning habits the bream can interbreed with the roach, but most hybrids retain the long anal fin, though sometimes it is a shorter version. Even so, it is much longer than that of the pure roach and is easily identified.

Bream are mainly bottom feeders and only come off the bottom to bask in the sun or in response to loose feed bait. They are shoal fish and some of these shoals can be of an incredible size, especially during the spawning season. Maggots, casters, worms, bread and seed baits will be taken by bream. They grow to a weight of up to 15 lbs in some waters, but most shoal fish are between 2 lbs and 4 lbs in weight, with the odd heavyweight being taken on occasions.

The Chub

Chub are a river fish, though some still waters can throw up the odd fish that have been stranded by receeding flood water, or that have been released by anglers using them as pike live baits.

Strangely, its the smaller rivers that produce the largest chub, although rich clean flowing rivers like the Severn and the Avon do occasionally produce the odd heavyweight. This is probably due to the easier fish location on the smaller waters. Even so, the upper reaches of large rivers and the smaller fertile rivers and streams do tend to be more prolific.

Due to its environment the chub is a very powerfully built streamlined fish, similar in colouring to the roach, but with a bronze tinge along the flanks. The large mouth of the chub will swallow just about any type of edible morsel, animal or vegetable. This can include crayfish, minnows, large black slugs, bread, worms, cheese, sausage and luncheon meat, maggots, casters and wasp grubs.

The larger fish tend to laze around in shady or sheltered parts of the river, in shoals of 4 or 5 fish. Almost every overhanging tree or bush on a good chub river will have its resident shoal. The smaller fish tend to congregate into larger shoals and patrol their various sections of the river in search of food. Good catches can be had on dull overcast days, but early morning and evening sessions, particularly in the summer months, seem to be the more rewarding, especially on clear waters.

When fishing for chub, especially in snaggy areas, good strong tackle is essential. Bread or worm baits can be used on size 8 or 6 hooks, tied directly to 5 lb B.S. line. Do not be afraid to use large baits when chub fishing. They generally produce far better results than small baits such as maggots. Chub tend to feed on sight, and a large bait is far more visible than a small one.

The Dace

The dace is also a river fish. They congregate in large shoals and patrol the shallow streamy areas of the river, feeding at all levels, but mainly around midwater and the surface. They are similar in appearance to small chub, but are thinner and not so heavy looking. They are silvery in appearance with very little colour in their fins. The fins also have a concave edge as opposed to the convex edge on the fins of the chub, particularly the anal fin, an important difference when trying to identify a dace from a small chub. They will take maggots, casters, bread and worms. The bites tend to be very fast and difficult to hit, especially in clear water.

The Bleak

A small silver fish found in both rivers and still waters. These are mainly surface feeders and can be a nuisance when fishing for bottom feeders such as roach and bream. They intercept the bait as it falls through the water, stripping or removing it from the hook before it can be got down to the bigger fish. Easily distinguished from the dace by its long shovel shaped bottom jaw.

The Barbel

One of the most powerful of our river fishes. The barbel is easily recognised by its dark bronze shape, its streamlined body and the four fleshy barbules, two being positioned either side of its mouth. These are used by the fish to locate its food by touch and smell as it roots around the river bed, from which it obtains most of its food supply. It prefers strong flowing water with a gravel bottom. Its streamlined shape allows it to hold its position in the most powerful of flows such as below weirs or waterfalls, or in the middle of strong flowing rivers.

It will take the majority of baits used by anglers, from maggots and worms to meat based pastes and luncheon meat.

Barbel can be caught using float fishing tactics but due to its normal habitats and the position of its mouth, legering tactics are the most successful.

The Gudgeon
Easily distinguishable from small barbel. The gudgeon has only two barbules, one either side of its mouth. This small fish is found in nearly all our rivers and stillwaters and is the biggest saver of dry nets that swims. Most anglers, whilst not appreciating its sporting qualities, which due to its smallness doesn't amount to very much, do appreciate the gudgeon's willingness to feed in almost all adverse conditions.

Many a winter match has been won by an odd couple of gudgeon on a day when no other species was caught.

They will accept any small bait such as maggots, casters, bits of worm and punched bread. They are brown in colour with a beautiful bluish tinge along their flanks and soft brown speckled fins.

The Carp
The largest and most powerful fish in our waters. There are four types of carp found in this country. The fully scaled common carp, the partly scaled mirror carp, the scaleless leather carp and the smaller but lively crucian carp.

With the exception of the crucian carp, these fish can be found in both still and flowing water. They are generally bronze in colour and have two barbules one either side of the mouth. The crucian carp has no barbules and thrives best in still waters. It seldom exceeds a couple of pounds in weight but gives a lively spirited scrap when hooked. It's a golden bronze in colour and is fully scaled. It has a deeper body than its big brothers and has very pretty red fins, sometimes with a slight purple tinge. The dorsal fin is very large and soft and it is a very attractive looking fish. Maggots, bread, sweetcorn and worms are the most popular baits.

The common carp is the largest of our carp, with the mirror and leather varieties quickly catching up with it in terms of growth potential. Most carp fisheries these days stock up with the fast growing strains of mirrors and leathers, and the fully scaled 'commons' are becoming less numerous.

The mirror carp is generally a shorter plumper fish than a common of the same weight. Instead of even rows of small scales as found on most of our fishes, the mirror carp has a couple of uneven rows of large scales centred around the lateral line and along the base of the dorsal fin. These irregular patterns vary from fish to fish, some being more heavily scaled than others.

The leather carp is of a similar appearance to the mirror carp in terms of shape and colouring, but is completely devoid of any scales at all. Occasionally an odd scale will appear near its tail, but normally is of a bare leathery appearance, hence the name.

Although they may all look different, their feeding habits and behaviour are the same. They are normally bottom feeders, but will often move and feed around the surface in conditions of hot weather and high water temperatures. During these periods, a lump of floating crust can attract fish that otherwise would not be interested in a bait presented normally on the bottom. When carp are feeding off the surface, loud clooping noises are given off by the fish as they suck in large mixtures of air, water and food. When bottom feeding, clouds of mud and bubbles are sent up by the fish rooting about in the bottom mud for bloodworm and other insect larvae.

On heavily fished waters, normal baits like bread, maggots and worms may not be very successful with the carp. Once they have been hooked they become very wary of these baits. Particle baits such as sweet corn may bring success over a limited period, but once the carp have become wary of these then your best way to succeed would be to start fishing with specials. These are made up of various combinations of ingredients. Pet foods, trout pellets, soya flour and wheatmeal flour, powdered milk and meat paté's are all used in various combinations to catch carp. Cheese and honey flavoured bread pastes are also popular. Many types of prepared specials and boilie's are now obtainable over the counter of most tackle shops.

Due to the immense strength of these fish, you should never attempt fishing for them without proper tackle. Your general purpose tackle will be adequate for fish up to two or three pounds in weight, but for the bigger fish, strong lines and large hooks together with the stronger test curve rods, must be used.

Water temperatures also play a large part in the feeding habits of carp. Although occasional carp are caught during the winter months by dedicated carp anglers, the fish tend to go off the feed during periods of low water temperature. I always feel a lot more confident when the water temperature is above 55°F. Below this, especially if a sudden drop in temperature has been experienced, the willingness of the carp to feed is greatly reduced.

The Tench

Like the carp, the tench feed better during periods of high water temperature. The tench is a beautiful olive green fish with very fine scales which are impossible to feel due to a thick coating of mucus. They have a very bright red eye and a small barbule either side of the mouth.

They are mainly bottom feeders and are immensely powerful when hooked.

As soon as the first frosts of winter are felt, the tench bury themselves under the mud and lie dormant until the spring. Occasionally fish are caught during the winter months, when water temperatures rise above the seasonal average, but generally speaking tench are a summer fish. They can be caught in flowing water, but they prefer ponds, lakes, drains and canals to the more swiftly flowing rivers.

Most baits will be taken by tench. Often when carp fishing, tench will snaffle your home made specials, much to the annoyance of the dedicated carp angler. Maggots, worms, bread and sweetcorn are the most popular baits. Tench tend to have a shorter memory than the carp, and never seem to 'go off' certain baits for more than a short period.

The Perch
Easily recognised by their green coloured body with black vertical stripes and double dorsal fin, perch are the smallest of our predatory species and can be caught on any live bait such as maggots, worms and minnows, or on small artificial lures.

They are found in still or flowing water, and feed in shoals. In the summer, large shoals of fish fry can be seen swimming along the shallow margins of the water, shadowed by a shoal of hungry perch.

In flowing waters, perch prefer to lie in the deeper more sheltered parts of the river, taking advantage of any cover such as weeds, rushes and bridge supports.

Small perch are very easy to catch and are very popular with anglers, due to their bright colours and uninhibited feeding habits.

The Ruffe or Pope
Similar to perch in their shape and fin structure, but differing in colour. Ruffe are a small fish and seldom reach more than a couple of ounces in weight. Unlike the perch, they are a short-sighted bottom feeder and their favourite baits are maggots and worms.

They are a light khaki brown in colour, with darker speckled markings. They are caught in still waters but are more often found in rivers.

The Pike
The king of predators. The pike relies almost solely on other fish as its main diet. Occasionally frogs, water voles, moorhens and chicks will be taken by the pike, which can be found in all waters from large rivers to the smallest ponds. Unlike the zander and perch, pike prefer a solitary life and tend to lie dormant in the cover of water weeds and rushes until their food comes to them. Then, with a powerful flick of their tails, they dart forward and seize their prey in their large jaws.

The dorsal fin of the pike is right at the end of its back near the tail. This gives the fish the added power needed for its sudden acceleration when attacking its prey from a standing start.

It is olive green in colour with pale yellow blotches along its flanks. Its jaws are large and powerful and great care must be taken when removing your hooks.

Dead baits such as herrings, spratts, roach and gudgeon should be used in preference to live baiting. Spinning lures, such as plugs and spoons are also excellent baits for pike, especially in large waters where vast areas need to be covered in search of the fish.

Never kill pike unnecessarily. Always use barbless hooks where possible and return the fish to the water with the minimum of delay.

The Zander

These fine sporting fish were introduced into this country from the continent in the 1960's. They are to be found in the Great Ouse system in Norfolk and Cambridgeshire. This includes the Relief Channel the river Delph and the connecting tributaries which run into the river Ouse.

It is silver in appearance with a light olive back. This colouring blends down into the flanks in the form of wide bars, similar to the stripes of the perch but not as prominent. Also like the perch it has two dorsal fins, the first being spiny followed by a softer fin. The fish is not related to the perch or the pike as many people assume. It is a separate species altogether.

The zander do not like a lot of direct light, so they tend to move more in the evening and early morning periods and at night. Unlike the pike, zander hunt their prey in the open water and tend to keep together in small shoals rather like wolf packs.

Small zander can be often caught on maggot and worm baits, whilst fishing for roach and bream. The larger fish are taken on scaled down pike tackle using small dead baits such as gudgeon, bleak and dace. Zander, like pike, have quite sharp teeth, so wire traces and snap tackle are also necessary.

The Eel

The eel is a commonly caught fish and is quite widespread in its distribution. It is very difficult to hold and hook removal is almost an impossibility, especially with the smaller ones. These will readily take maggots and worms that are fished on or close to the bottom.

Large eels are caught by fishing small dead baits such as gudgeon and bleak. They generally feed at night and still waters are the holding places of the really large ones. The snaggier the area the more likely it is that a large eel is around.

Wire traces again are needed, if the larger specimens are to be landed successfully. They fight very hard and if allowed to get in amongst snags it's almost impossible to get them out.

8 WATERCRAFT & TACKLE HANDLING

Many of the functions carried out by an experienced angler are done automatically without him thinking about them. Assembling the tackle, casting and retrieving, playing fish, all these things are done instinctively. When an experienced angler retrieves his tackle he knows, without consciously looking, when to stop winding, so that when he lifts his rod, his hook will swing straight into his hand without him having to reach out or release line from his reel.

When hooking a large fish, the experienced angler will release the back wind or anti-reverse lever, in order to give the fish line if necessary and he will know just when to stop winding and to lean back with the rod to draw the fish over the rim of the landing net.

Inexperienced anglers have to learn these things; they have to think and look at every function. A lot of things will soon come naturally, other things will never be done right unless a conscious effort is made to overcome any bad habits. Many anglers go through their whole lives making things awkward for themselves, because they do not know, or have not been shown the correct way of doing things. Also, they do not enjoy their fishing as much, because they are forever getting into tangles, breaking tackle or losing fish and cannot understand why.

If you can master these things, so that you also do them automatically without thinking, you will then be on the path to successful angling. To explain these various points, I am going to go through a typical fishing session. We will look at what has to be done, the order in which it should be done, and most important of all, why it must be done and what will happen if it is not done. If you can learn this and follow it to the letter, every time you go fishing, you will rapidly become an accomplished angler.

First of all, before you even set off out of the house, you must check over your tackle to ensure you have packed everything you will need for the particular water you are going to fish. Check for essential items such as hooks, nets, bait and your hook disgorger. Make sure you are dressed adequately for the conditions you are likely to be fishing in; you can never put on too much clothing. If you get too hot you can take some off, but you cannot put on what you haven't got if the weather turns nasty.

On arriving at the waterside, do not just make a beeline for the nearest vacant swim. Study the water and assess where the most probable area is that the fish will be, relative to the prevailing conditions. It is no good finding a nice sheltered spot if all the fish are at the other end of the water. In cold conditions the fish tend to move into the deeper areas of the water. If this means you have to fish with the wind in your face, then this you must do if you want to catch fish. Obviously if you have a choice of good fishing areas, you will want to fish where you will be the most comfortable. But learning to fish in adverse conditions is essential if you want to be successful. So don't look for comfort and make that a greater priority than catching fish.

If you know your water well and you know the areas that produce in various conditions, all well and good, but if the water you intend to fish is relatively new to you, then a few minutes looking for likely fish holding areas is time well spent.

Fish do not hang around certain areas of a water because it looks nice and cosy. They are in these areas because they offer a combination of shelter and food. In flowing water, natural obstructions such as weeds, rocks and bends are all attractive to various species. Some like roach and bream will tend to stay in the deeper slacker water, whilst dace will favour the shallow streamy parts.

Chub and barbel tend to lie up in the deeper areas during the daytime, but will move into the shallower streamy areas at night and various parts of the day when conditions are favourable to them. Natural rivers that alter in depth and flow and that twist and turn, will hold more varied features than a man made drain, which is uniform in width and depth and has little bankside vegetation. Fish location on these types of water is very much a matter of chance, or knowledge of the hot spots.

Locating fish in natural rivers is much easier. Deep holes can be seen if the river is clear or they can be found by plumbing in cloudy water. The outside of a bend will be deeper due to the force of the current hitting it and scouring out a channel when in winter spate (see Fig. 17). Obstructions such as weed beds, tree roots and bridge supports are all good fish holding areas, as are the bottoms of weirs and waterfalls, especially in the warmer weather when they provide much needed oxygen in the water.

Chub are very fond of shady tree lined areas. Most rivers that contain chub will have a resident shoal under overhanging branches, especially if this occurs over a deeper slacker area of water. In weirpools you will find dace and barbel in the stronger water with bream and roach lying in the slacker water at the edge of the pool. Perch are very likely in these slacker areas too, lying in wait for the minnow and fry shoals to appear. Naturally the areas that attract fish also attract the predators that feed on them, such as Pike and Eels.

In streamy water, if you want to locate a shoal of Dace, carry a few floating maggot chrysalids with you. By walking downstream throwing a few of these in every couple of yards or so, you will soon know where the dace are by the fish rising to the chrysalids. Once they have been located, sit well above them and start feeding in samples of your bait a few at a time at regular intervals, then trot your tackle downstream to the fish.

On still waters, weedbeds are the main holding areas of fish during the daytime. In the early mornings the fish will patrol the margins of the lake or pond (see Fig. 18), gradually moving out into the deeper water as the sun rises. Shelves and gulleys are favourite haunts of fish, as are sandy or gravel bars. In large featureless waters such as reservoirs, fish location can be a matter of chance and only observation or local knowledge can assist you in these circumstances.

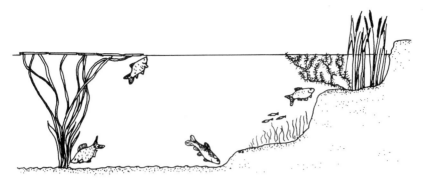

Fig. 16. Shelves and Ledges.

You have selected your swim and you are eager to tackle up and get started. The normal impulse is to get out the rod, tackle it up and get fishing. You must try to control this impulse at all times, because it is here that your first problems will occur. If you do this you will find that when you have tackled up you will have nowhere to put the rod whilst you set up the rest of your equipment. Nowhere that is except for the bank. If a rod is laid on the bank whilst you are still moving about getting prepared there is a strong risk of treading on it and breaking it or someone else doing it for you. Never leave a rod on the bank, for even if it does avoid being trodden on, the chances are that the line will get tangled up in the grass or other such obstructions. The correct way to get tackled up is as follows.

First of all you put down your tackle well back from the water's edge. This is especially important if you intend to fish at close range. Remove all the items you will be likely to need from your basket and holdall and lay them neatly together. Assemble your rod rests and stick them in the bank well clear of the waters edge and any pathways or obstructions, also assemble your landing net and keepnet. You can now put your rod together. There is a right way and a wrong way to do this. Do it the wrong way and you are struggling and risk damaging it. The correct way to assemble a rod is as follows. Remove the top piece from the bag only. Then fit this into the ferrule or spigot of the centre section (this is assuming it is a 3 piece rod). The centre section should still be in the rod bag. Line up the rings and then remove the now assembled top and centre piece from the bag. You then fit it to the butt section, again leaving it in the bag. Line up the butt ring with the other rings and then draw the bag off of the butt section and you are then left with the assembled rod. The reason you do not take all the pieces out of the bag together is that if you do this, they get rattled against each other and this will result in chipped varnish and bent or damaged rings (see Fig. 20).

You then put the empty rod bag into your basket and place the rod safely onto the ready positioned rod rests, making sure that the tip is not vulnerable to passers by walking into it.

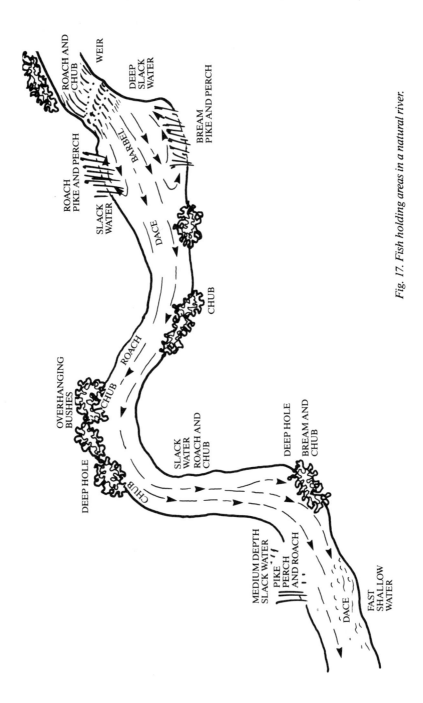

Fig. 17. Fish holding areas in a natural river.

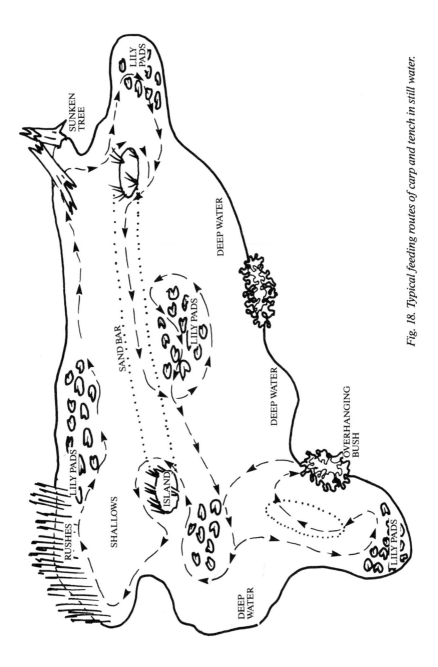

Fig. 18. Typical feeding routes of carp and tench in still water.

You now fit on the reel. This should be fitted as far up the handle as possible (see Fig. 21) otherwise the rod will be out of balance and feel top heavy. When the rod is held with your hand around the reel, several inches of handle should protrude past your elbow (see Fig. 22). Now with the rod still on the rod rest, open the bale arm on the reel and thread the line through the rings taking care not to miss any out. You then pull the line down until it is level with the reel and engage the pickup.

You now select the float which is the correct one for the conditions prevailing and the distance at which you intend to fish and fix it onto the line at the approximate depth you consider the swim to be. You then tie on your hook length and shot up the float to its correct pattern.

If you are legering, you fit whatever indicator you are intending to use onto the rod tip before assembling the rod.

After your terminal tackle has been prepared you then slot the hook into the reel fitting (see Fig. 21) and take up any slack line. You can now put the rod onto the rod rests whilst you prepare your swim.

Fig. 19. Fish being swung to hand.

Fig. 20. Assembling a rod the correct way.

REEL FITTED AS
NEAR TO THE TOP OF
HANDLE AS POSSIBLE

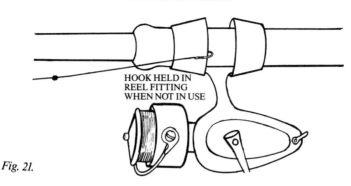

HOOK HELD IN
REEL FITTING
WHEN NOT IN USE

Fig. 21.

If you are to fish in flowing water which has a bit of colour in it, or at long range on flowing or still water, then a standing position is normally the best. This allows you to control your tackle better. If you are fishing at close range or on a clear water where a standing position is either unnecessary or liable to frighten the fish, then a sitting position should be adopted.

The first thing to do after you have assembled all your equipment is to position your basket or seat. It wants to be far enough back from the edge of the bank to allow you a good foothold, but not so far back as to make it necessary for you to stand up to land fish and put them in the keepnet. Once everything is in position you should not have to stand or move around at anytime during the session except when needing extra reach to control a sizeable fish in weedy or snaggy swims (see Figs. 23 and 24).

The basket or seat should be stable. It must not be liable to tilt or move about. Always carry a small trowel with you to use if necessary.

Once this has been achieved, you must then remove any snags around the area where your rod is to be positioned. Again moderation is the key. Do not go ripping out or flattening vast expanses of bankside growth or rushes. You want to retain as much natural cover as possible. All you need to do is ensure that your reel and line will not snag on anything whilst it is being held. Be as quiet as possible whilst carrying out these necessary tasks. Take care to keep low down and not to bump about on the bank. Never allow yourself to be silhouetted against the skyline and keep all movements slow and careful.

Once the preparations have been carried out and your seat is positioned, you can now move your rod and rod rests into position next to your seat and position your keep net and landing net, ensuring they can be reached without leaving your basket. Always position your rod rests so that the rod tip is as close to the surface of the water as possible. Do not follow the bad example shown on television or in catalogue adverts, where anglers are shown sitting with their rods pointing up in the air at a 45° angle. Remember these people are not anglers, they are actors or models being filmed to advertise products.

They are not there to catch fish and would not catch fish with their rods set at this ridiculous angle.

Bait tins and tackle containers are also positioned within easy reach. You can now put any items you will not be needing back into your basket and holdall. You then put your holdall and tackle box within your side vision, especially if fishing in a crowded place.

Unfortunately, this is not a perfect world and you stand a strong risk of having your hard earned tackle stolen while you are concentrating on your float or tip, so don't leave loose tackle behind you.

If you are to fish in a standing position, a bait bag or apron is a very handy item to have. These are easily made up out of a scrap piece of material. They hang around the neck by a strap, allowing you to feed without having to bend down each time. Also they are an obvious advantage when wading in a shallow river or stream.

Before you start to fish you still have one very important thing to do. You must accurately plumb the depth (see Fig. 40). If you intend to fish at fairly close range on a pond, lake or river, you need to find the shelf. This can be a single shelf or series of shelves and you will need to find the exact position of these before you start to feed. Fish always tend to feed along these shelves (see Fig. 16).

Once you have set your tackle to the depth you are going to fish and noted the whereabouts of any shelves or ledges, you can now throw in a couple of pinches of loose feed or one or two small balls of groundbait. If after a half hour or so you have not had any bites, the worse thing to do is to start throwing in any more loose bait. When the fish do find their way into the swim, the bait will be just lying in an untouched pile on the bottom. The chances of the fish finding your hookbait amongst this lot is very slim. The fish will quickly fill up and then leave the swim with half of the bait and your hookbait still lying there untouched.

If on the other hand if bites are forthcoming almost immediately, then a pinch of loose feed every couple of minutes or so should keep the fish in the area. Notice I said a pinch of feed. If maggots or seed baits are being used this will consist of a half dozen samples. If you scoop up the bait in your hand, as opposed to taking a pinch between your fingers, you will find you have 30-50 samples. Throw this lot in every few minutes and you will soon over feed the fish and your bites will stop. You want to hold the interest of the fish over an extended period. This can only be done by light, regular feeding.

When fishing flowing water, a pinch of feed can be thrown upstream of your float on every cast, so it is constantly being swept downstream by the current.

Fig. 22. Correctly holding a rod and reel.

Sometimes you may start to catch fish regularly, then suddenly the bites cease. Many anglers just sit back thinking that the fish have 'gone off' and do nothing to find out why. One of the reasons the bites have stopped may be that the fish have moved up in the water to intercept the loose feed. This is a quite common occurrence, especially when fishing in flowing water. The fish, as they move upstream towards the angler, also move up in the water following the path of the falling food.

Experienced anglers are able to judge by the depth of the swim and the speed of the current just whereabouts down the swim the loose feed will hit the bottom. If they start to catch fish at the tail end of the swim and then progressively closer and the bites slow down as the fish reach the estimated area, they will automatically 'shorten off' by moving their float closer to the hook, thereby keeping 'in touch' with the fish. They may also 'lighten off' by moving some of the shot up towards the float to give a more natural fall of the hookbait to simulate the fall of the loose feed (see Fig. 25).

Always try to think what effect your feeding is having on the fish and try to emulate this with your hookbait as well as prevailing conditions will allow. The ability to learn this will set you apart from the average angler; an essential progression if you have ambitions towards match fishing or just wish to be a very competent angler.

When fishing at close to medium range, an underhand or side cast is the best way of casting. As well as being smoother it also allows the tackle to enter the water with the minimum of disturbance. Overhead casting at close range is untidy and unnecessary. To cast underhand, you hold the line just above the hook in your left hand (assuming we are right handed). You then point the rod forward and downward. Then with a smooth upward movement of the rod you swing the tackle outward and release the line. As the tackle nears the surface of the water, you allow the end of the rod to lower. The best way to practice this method of casting is to tie a small weight to the end of your line.

Fig. 23. Equipment layout for fishing in seated position.

Fig. 24. Equipment layout for fishing in standing position.

Fig. 25. Fish rising in the water in response to loose feed.

You can then practice casting either at the waterside or on your lawn or in your local park.

When casting overhead, the most common fault is to lower the rod tip too far whilst the tackle is in the air. Force yourself to stop the downwards movement of the rod when casting. The rod should not be lowered more than 45 degrees from the vertical if a smooth long cast and gentle entry of the tackle into the water is to be achieved (see Fig. 26). As the tackle nears the surface, the line coming off the reel should be 'feathered'. This is done by slowing the rate at which the line is coming off the spool with your finger. By doing this, the terminal tackle will be straightened out, eliminating tangles and allowing the bait to fall through the water in a nice straight line ready to indicate a bite at anytime.

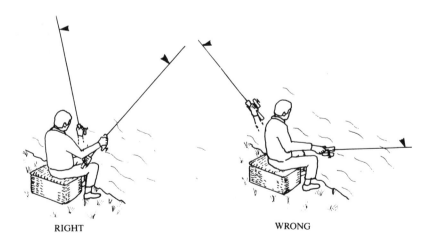

RIGHT   WRONG

Fig. 26. Overhead casting.

It takes a lot of practice before this is achieved properly. It is all a question of feel. When you first try to feather your line you will probably be a bit heavy handed and cause the line to snatch and jerk the tackle. Do not be put off if this happens. Keep practising and the correct feel will soon be developed.

When a bite is indicated by your float or bite indicator, you must strike to set the hook into the fish's mouth. This operation should be done by moving the rod in a fast smooth upwards or sideways direction until the fish is felt. Then, the force of the strike should be cut off, otherwise you may snap your hooklength or rip the lip of the fish. Again only practice and experience will teach you how to strike correctly and many breakages will occur before you learn to curtail your enthusiasm for over striking.

Do not confuse speed with snatching. Always strike down the line with a smooth sweeping action. Once the fish is felt, keep the rod well up to allow the curve of the rod tip to absorb the shock caused by the lunges of the fish. This is the job of the rod tip, not the line. Always have the slipping clutch or drag set to below the breaking strain of the hook length.This will help prevent breaking the strike or if the fish runs directly away from you.

If you are playing a good sized fish, move your anti-reverse lever to the off position. If the fish runs, you can give line by allowing the reel to wind backwards using your finger against the head of the reel to control it. This is by far the best and most sensitive method of playing fish when using a fixed spool reel. The anti-reverse lever should always be in the 'on' position except when playing fish. Otherwise, when you strike, the reel will spin round in reverse causing either a tangle or your hook not to penetrate the fish's mouth. Learn to operate this lever without having to look down or fumble for it. If the anti-reverse lever is difficult to reach or operate when you are buying a new reel, avoid that reel.

The next problem most inexperienced anglers come up against is retrieving their tackle. It is amazing how reluctant anglers are to hold their rods up in a vertical or near vertical position. Failure to do this contributes to more tangles and broken lines than any other reason. If you hold the rod in a horizontal position when retrieving your tackle, you are more likely to get your hook or line caught in weeds or obstructions. Also you are unable to judge when to stop winding so that your hook length will swing into your hand. If you wind in too far your float will either bang against the top ring causing probable damage to either the ring or the float, or your tackle will be out of reach and vulnerable to tangles whilst you fumble with your reel to lower it down again. With the rod held well up you can control and steer your tackle around any obstructions. An essential function, especially when bringing in a fish.

When you are netting a large fish you must always leave enough length of line to keep the fish in the water whilst you lean back with your rod to bring it over the net. A common fault with young and novice anglers is to play the fish with the rod almost horizontal, then find they cannot draw the fish into the net without releasing line again to allow them to raise the rod to a vertical position without lifting the fish out of the water. More sizeable fish are lost at the net through this reason than by any other.

You will often see pictures in the angling press of matchmen in the process of netting a good fish. Their rods are always held well up and high into the air whilst performing this delicate operation. This is so that if the fish makes a sudden lunge, they can lower their arm to give line, but still maintain a near vertical position with the rod, allowing them to control the fish with the minimum of stress being put onto the line and the hook hold. Too much pressure at this point with the line at such an acute angle to the rod will cause the hook to pull out and the loss of a possible match winning fish.

Matchmen do this by instinct. They know just by the feel how much pressure they can exert at this point. Novice anglers have got to learn this by experience. Never fall into the trap of thinking 'Oh we got a big one on here, let's get it in quickly before we lose it'. If you do not control this natural urge to panic when you see the fish rolling in front of you, then the result will be a lot of lost fish.

Take your time and make sure the fish is played out before you attempt to net it. When you come to net it, keep its head above the water, sink the landing net under the surface and draw the fish over it by leaning backwards with the rod. Once the fish is over the net, gently lift the net and the fish out of the water. If as you are about to lift the net, the fish lunges away, quickly lower the net and the rod and play it a little longer before repeating the operation. Never lunge or stab forward with the net. Never try to pull a still struggling fish over it. A little self discipline and calmness at this point will be rewarded by the banking of a good fish.

Breaking down your tackle is the exact reverse of the assembly process. Never put your tackle away wet. If it has been raining, wipe your rod and reel down before putting them away and then dry them out thoroughly when you get home. Always carry an old towel in your basket for this purpose.

Always check around your swim before you leave to make sure you have not left any rod rests or other items. Also pick up any litter. This is very important. Never leave hook packets, loose line or plastic bags at the waterside. Loose line can inflict terrible injuries and a lingering death to birds and wildlife. Never throw away a hook with the bait still attached to it. Any left over bait that you will not be using should be taken home to be disposed of or, if only a small amount, throw it up the bank for the birds. Never throw large quantities of bait or ground bait into the water after you have finished fishing. Never leave bait to go stale in your bait containers. Wipe out or wash your bait containers after use, making sure the air holes are not blocked up with mud or sawdust. Hang your keepnets and landing nets up to dry. Be very careful where you store them. Mice love the flavour of keepnets and can chew a lot of very large holes in a net in a very short time. So if you keep your tackle in a shed or garage, especially in the winter months, keep them out of the reach of any rodents. The best way is to hang them from a peg in the wall, well clear of shelves or ledges. Waders are best hung up unfolded or cracks can appear along the folds. A little thought in the care and maintenance of your equipment will save you pounds in replacement costs later on.

9 FLOATS AND SHOTTING

I consider this next chapter to be one of the most important parts of this book. If the contents of it are fully digested and understood by the reader, then he or she will hold the key to successful angling and will avoid a large majority of the pitfalls laid in the path of newcomers to the sport.

I have aimed to keep it as simple and as uncomplicated as possible. Once these basic principles have been mastered, then the more complex set ups will become a natural progression. For the purpose of catching fish, the basic set ups described in this chapter will cover all but the most extreme of situations.

Before I get on to the subject of floats, I think it is important to understand a few things about split shot. As with other items of fishing tackle, they vary in quality but not so much in price. The cost of good shot is seldom any more than the cost of rubbish. Although they may be classed by the trade as 'sundry items', they perform a very important function.

Most inexperienced anglers assume that the sole function of shot is to cock the float and provide enough weight for casting. This is where they succumb to the largest of pitfalls.

The purpose of split shot, together with the float, is to present the bait to the fish in a manner that is natural and acceptable to them in the prevailing conditions, at the same time indicating through the float that the bait has been taken by a fish. By altering a shots position or size, or by changing the type or size of the float, we can alter the presentation of the bait or the way in which a bite is indicated. So the split shot is a very important item of tackle, just as important as the float, as each are dependent upon the other. So, how can we avoid bad shot, or more to the point, how do we recognise bad shot so we know what to avoid.

Bad shot is hard and will not close around the line without a lot of pressure, which in turn causes damage to the line. Good shot is soft. It will close with either finger pressure or just a gentle squeeze with either your teeth or shot pliers. Also it can be opened by just pressing your nail into the slot when you want to remove it or move it to another position on your line.

Bad shot can also have the slot cut too deep, too shallow or off centre, they can also vary in size or weight or be an odd size.

Most bad shot come in segmented plastic containers known in the trade as shot dispensers. Avoid these types of containers. They are generally unmarked as to the size of shots they contain. Also if you drop them as a lot of anglers do whilst struggling to eject a shot out of them without a load coming out at once, they invariably roll down the bank into the water and then all your shots are lost.

The best shots come in either packets or in spill proof containers which hold just one individual size. If you buy your shots in this way, the initial outlay may be slightly more, but you will get more shots for your money, they will be of a better quality and you will be able to identify the sizes, which is very important.

The sizes are as follows, starting from the largest and working downwards in size:— S.S.G. (Swan shot) A.A.A., B.B., Nos. 1, 2, 3, 4, 5, 6, 7, 8. (Dust shot). 10, 12, 13 (Micro Dust shots). Apart from the lettered shots, the difference between the numbered shot sizes is very small and you do not need them all. The sizes I use and the sizes I recommend you to use should be as follows: S.S.G., A.A.A., B.B., Nos. 4, 6 and 8. Each one is approximately half the size of the previous shot, i.e. 2 A.A.A. = 1 swan. 2 B.B. = 1 A.A.A., 2 Nos. 4 = 1 B.B., and so on. These sizes will more than cover all your shotting requirements for general float fishing with rod and reel.

The sizes 10, 12, 13 (Micro dust) are generally only used when fishing with a roach pole. They are very tiny and are difficult to put on at the bank side. I will cover these sizes in the chapter on Pole fishing.

When you buy a float from a shop, it will sometimes have the shot loading on the stem. It may say 3 A.A.A., or 2 B.B., or 5 No. 6. This does not mean that you put just these shots onto the line. This is only to indicate the approximate total shot loading capacity of the float. In the case of the 2 B.B. float, you may split it up into 3 No. 4 and 2 No. 6, or string out 2 No. 4, 3 No. 6 and 2 No. 8's depending on the conditions and the type of bait presentation required. This will be covered later on. The important thing is to get fixed in your mind the difference in the sizes and how they relate to each other.

One last but important word about lead shot. It has been suggested that large numbers of swans are dying of lead poisoning after picking up and swallowing shots whilst feeding on the bottom of rivers and lakes. It is important not to discard used shot by throwing it into the water. Always re-use shot as often as possible and take any unusable shot home to be disposed of.

It is currently being proposed that from January 1987, the manufacture of all lead shots and weights from No. 6 upwards to 2 ozs will be banned. Number 8 and micro-dust will still be available in lead.

If passed, this law will apply to the manufacture of lead weights. The rules applying to its use will vary from one water to another, depending upon the owners. Some will impose a total ban on lead, but most will follow the government guidelines.

Many patterns of lead free alternative weights are now available. These include hinged tungston shot, stainless steel coils, and a putty that can be molded to any shape for use as leger weights or shot. One company has produced a lead free alternative that looks and performs the same as lead shot. They are slightly larger and lighter than their lead equivalents, and are as soft as the better quality lead shot. I consider them to be the better of the current lead free alternatives in performance and reliability, and in the fact that myself and other writers on angling will not have to completely re-write the textbooks on the subject.

Now to the floats. They come in dozens of shapes and sizes, all of which is very confusing to the novice. Modern floats are very good compared to the limited selection we had to choose from when I started fishing. The last 10 years has seen vast improvements in the materials and quality of commercial floats, but unfortunately there is still a lot of rubbish being made by firms who refuse to progress and move with the times. So as the earlier chapters say, let's get the stuff we do not want out of the way first.

Do not buy brightly coloured floats with big bulbous bodies. For some reason novice anglers are drawn like flies to this type of float. Avoid them at all costs. They may look nice but they will not help you to catch fish. Avoid floats that have more than 12 mm of colour on the tip, or that are painted in a multiple of different colours. If you keep to the patterns of floats that are described in this chapter and avoid any other type you will not go far wrong. Before you buy a float, think to yourself what type of water is it designed for? Does it do a specific job? Can it do what I want it to do, and most important of all, do I need it?

Floats fall into two main categories. Stillwater floats and flowing water floats (or trotting floats). If we can separate the two types completely from each other then we will be half way there. The number of times I have seen anglers using stick floats connected to the line bottom end only, whilst fishing a pond is countless. Admittedly they get bites, but they would get a lot more if they had the right float on. They could control the tackle and not have it drifting about so much, all of which limits your chances of getting a bite. Some floats like the straight peacock or waggler type floats can be used in either still or flowing water as will be explained, but generally speaking if the buoyancy of a float, i.e. the main body of the float is at the bottom, then it is a stillwater float. If it is near the top then it is a trotting float. If it is the same all along as with a straight peacock, then it can be used as either. But the shotting pattern in each case will be different. So, how do you decide which float to use? What are the things to consider when we choose our floats? The main rules are these: The type of water. Is it still or is it flowing? The range at which we are to fish. The depth of the water. The direction and the strength of the wind. These are the four main considerations.

Let's first look at fishing in a small pond. It is a nice fine day, there is not much of a breeze and the surface of the pond is still, flat and unruffled. The swim you have chosen is about 5ft deep, and you are going to fish just over the marginal weed up to a rod and a half out. What float do you use? Well you only need a small float, as you are not going to cast very far.

It must also be light, so as to land gently on the water with the minimum of disturbance. I would choose one of two types, either a peacock quill with a thin cane or peacock insert, or a reversed crow quill. This is made from a crow quill as the name implies, which has been up-ended, i.e. the fat end of the quill is at the bottom. The floats are connected to the line by the bottom ring only with a shot on each side of the ring locking it to the line. You then put a No. 8 Dust shot 18″ above the hook and a No. 6 shot 24″ above that, any more shot required to set the tip so that only ⅛″ (3 mm) approximately is showing, is placed up against the lower locking shot (see Fig. 27).

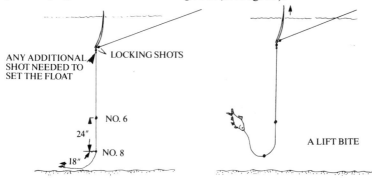

ANY ADDITIONAL SHOT NEEDED TO SET THE FLOAT

LOCKING SHOTS

NO. 6

24″

NO. 8

18″

A LIFT BITE

Fig. 27.

Note that the No. 8 Shot is set a couple of inches off the bottom with the hook length lying on the bottom. This is the normal method of fishing this type of water. When a fish takes the bait the float will do one of two things. It will go under or it will lift sharply. If it lifts it means the fish has picked up the bait and is also lifting the bottom shot. This is just as good a bite as when the float goes under, so strike.

When the float is cast in you will see the two shots acting on the float. The tip will be sticking up perhaps an inch or so at first, then as the No. 6 shot settles it will pull the tip down to its first setting. Then, as the No. 8 shot settles it will lower again to the 3 mm setting. Count in your mind how long it takes between these settings. If they are delayed, strike. This means a fish has taken the bait on the way down and is holding up the shots. If this happens a few times and you are not connecting with the fish but your bait is being sucked, lower your float so that the bait is just off the bottom. This is called shortening off. It will give you a more positive indication of a bite if the fish are taking 'on the drop'. Also, you could move the indicating shot closer to the hook to achieve the same result.

Let us now imagine that you are fishing the same swim, but the breeze gets stronger and the water is rippling up. It is causing your line to 'BOW' and it is drifting and pulling your float away from the baited area. How do you combat this and keep the float in one place? Firstly you do what is called back shotting.

This means that you split one of the locking shots into two smaller shots, i.e. if one of the locking shots is a B.B., you take it off and replace it with two No. 4's.

Fig. 28. Preventing drift in windy conditions.

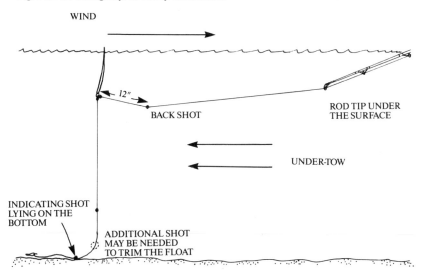

You put one No. 4 back where you took the B.B. shot from, and then put the other No. 4 12″ back up the line towards the rod end. This is to help sink the line under the surface away from the wind (see Fig. 28). When you cast in again, you cast several feet further out than you were before. Then you put the rod tip under the surface and give a couple of quick turns of the reel. This will pull the line under the water out of the way of the wind. You then position the rod so that the tip is just under the surface. When you get a bite you strike as normal.

If the float you are using is fairly heavy, then you may have enough weight to pull against to sink the line, without needing to back shot. Another dodge used by anglers to make their line sink, is to run the line through a cloth soaked with washing up liquid. This takes the glaze off the line and helps it to sink.

If the wind is so strong that the tackle is still drifting, this may be due to undertow as well as wind. In other words, your tackle may be moving in the opposite direction to the wind due to the undertow of the water, which on some waters is very strong. Then you may have to move your indicating shot so that it is lying hard on the bottom. This is best done by moving your float up a foot as opposed to moving the shot down. You may then need to add another No. 8 to the line so that it is just off the bottom. This is because your original shot being hard on the bottom, is not acting on the float. Sometimes, the addition of another shot is not necessary as the force of the 'pull" of the water is enough to lower the float tip and the addition of another shot in this case may mean it will pull the float under, giving you a 'false bite'. In these situations it's a case of trial and error until you get it working properly.

Now let us suppose that you are fishing the same pond, but you want to fish further out. There may be a patch of weed or lily-pads in the middle of the pond, and you have reason to believe that there are fish feeding around them. The two floats I have described are not heavy enough to cast out that far comfortably, so we need a float that is heavier but just as sensitive. We could use a longer or thicker peacock quill that will take more shot, or you could use a float of the same length but with a balsa body to increase the weight.

Fig. 29. Stillwater floats. Close and medium range.

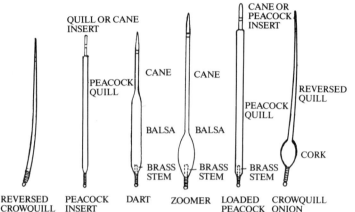

You will not want any more weight down the line than the No. 6 and No. 8 but you can put bigger locking shots around the float, or, you use a 'loaded' float, i.e. a float that has some weight built into the stem. There are three types of floats that could be suitable, the dart, the zoomer or the loaded peacock. The dart is a float with a slim balsa body with a cane antenna and a brass stem. The zoomer is of the same materials but has a fatter, shorter balsa body and a longer, thicker antenna. The loaded peacock is like the peacock insert but is made of thicker quill or is longer, and has a brass stem (see Fig. 29).

The same terminal tackle is used as with the lighter floats and the same principles apply in windy conditions. Care must be taken when casting these heavier floats as they are prone to splash if they hit the water with too much force. A side or underhand cast is preferable to a overhead cast. With practice an underhand cast can give you just as much range as an overhead cast and if you can get the hang of it, it comes in very handy if you have to fish in a swim with overhanging trees or thick bushes immediately behind you.

So for medium or close range fishing on still waters these are all you will need. They will cope with most conditions in waters up to 8 ft deep and distances of up to 20 yards or so.

For larger and deeper still waters like the Fen drains, or rivers like the Welland or Nene which have little or no flow, a heavier range of floats are called for. These are stepped up versions of the zoomer and peacock floats, with the exception of the antenna or wind-beater type. These have an antenna made from cane or fibreglass. As these materials are non-buoyant it allows you to have much more of the float sticking out of the water, a necessity when fishing in a strong wind when the waves are several inches high (Fig. 30).

Fig. 30. Still water floats for long range or deep water.

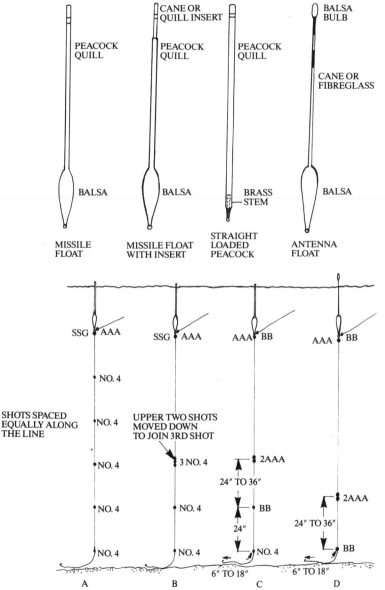

Fig. 31. Various ways of shotting a 2SSG float.

The shotting patterns for these floats are also stepped up. More weight is needed down the line to get the bait down to the fish quickly and to hold the floats stable in a strong wind. The indicating shot also has to be bigger. Due to the increased thickness of the peacock a No. 4 at least will be needed to indicate a lift bite. If it becomes really necessary to use a No. 8 or No. 6 shot due to shy bites, then a float with a fine peacock or cane insert must be used. In waters up to 8 ft deep, a strung out pattern normally performs the best. This will indicate bites at all depths and will allow you to shuffle the shots about if a faster drop is needed (Fig. 31A).

For example, if you are fishing with 5 No. 4 shots strung out and the fish are taking near the bottom, the top two shots can be moved down to join the third one. This will give you a faster initial drop with the bottom half still falling at the same rate (see Fig. 31B). If the tackle is drifting badly in the wind and you want to fish off the bottom, then you can reduce the locking shot size and put more shot down the line with the bulk shots. This will give you more stability (see Fig. 31C). When using the cane or fibreglass antenna float, use a B.B. shot as the indicator if possible, as this will act on several inches of the antenna, giving a pronounced lift or sinking of the 1″ or so of tip protruding (Fig. 31D). Stepped down versions of the illustrated shotting patterns can also be used on the medium range of floats when conditions require it.

When using floats with a large shot carrying capacity of 2 S.S.G. or more, a heavier mainline must be used to reduce the chances of snapping on the cast or the strike. Use a line of 3-3½ lb B.S. instead of 2-2½ lb normally used when fishing. When fishing with small hooks, finer hook lengths can still be used in proportion to the hook size, as shown on the chart of recommended line strength to hook size.

The reason I recommend the use of locking shots to hold the floats in position, as opposed to looping the line through the float ring several times, is because if you loop the line, when you adjust the position of the float either upwards or downwards it causes the line to curl or kink, which as well as inviting tangles also weakens the line.

Opponents of the locking shots on the other hand say that there is as much chance of damaging the line by moving shots up and down, or by just putting shots on the line in the first place. They have a point! If you use hard shots as opposed to soft shots, then line damage is a strong possibility. But if soft shot is used and carefully closed onto the line with just finger pressure, then no problems should evolve. Care must also be used when moving shots up and down the line. Always if possible open the shots with your thumb nail before repositioning them. If they are to be slid just an inch or so, just crack the slot open enough to allow the shot to slide freely, then wet the line with a bit of spit and slide the shot slowly to its new position. Never slide shot about quickly as this will cause weakening of the line due to the friction produced by the shot and the line rubbing together. There are several ways of enabling a fast change of float when fishing bottom end only. The most common is to employ a very small link swivel (see Fig. 32).

This method has the advantage in that all stillwater floats have an eye of some sort at the base and most eyes will clip onto the swivel. The disadvantage with this method is that the occasional tangle occurs with the line wrapping around either the swivel or getting trapped in the clip.

Fig. 32. Quick change float attachments.

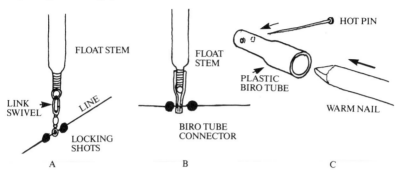

A more foolproof method is the use of plastic ball point pen refills. A half inch is cut off an old ball point refill and the top ⅔ are opened out by pressing in a warm nail. A hot pin is then pushed through the bottom ⅓ of the tube to allow the line to be threaded through. As I make most of my own floats, I always fit a stem of 2 mm cane or brass onto which I whip an eye. Most shop bought darts and wagglers are also fitted with this size of stem. So if you adopt this method from the beginning and buy or make your floats with a 2 mm stem, all or most of your floats will fit snugly and firmly into the opened out tube and float changes can be performed in a matter of seconds without breaking down the terminal tackle. Don't worry about the floats flying out of the tube on the cast. I have used this method for several seasons now and I have not lost a float yet.

Some of the larger wagglers and antenna floats have 3 mm stems. These can be accommodated in the plastic tubing used to areate fish tanks. I always carry several sizes with me to cover all eventualities. This method is also a boon when using a sliding float. A method of float fishing in deep water that will be dealt with in a later chapter covering advanced techniques.

A commercially made silicon version of these attachments in several sizes are now available from tackle shops.

Floats for Rivers and Streams

Many and varied are the types of floats for moving water, just as the waters themselves are many and varied. From the slow moving uniform characteristics of the fen drain, to the clear sparkling Yorkshire spate rivers, that can vary in depth, flow, width and direction a dozen times in just a one mile stretch.

To try and cover all the aspects of fishing in moving water thoroughly, would be a time consuming task for me and would be very confusing to you inexperienced anglers, trying to sort out which part of it applies to your particular waters.

As in the previous section on still water floats, I will cover a basic selection of floats that will cope with most of the situations anglers are likely to come up against.

As with still water floats, a number of rules apply to the selection of the correct type of float for the conditions on the day. If these are learnt and applied you will not go far wrong, and your ultimate aim of catching fish will be fulfilled.

The conditions governing the choice of float on flowing waters are these:— The speed of the flow, is it gentle, medium or fast? The direction of the wind, is it upstream, downstream or across? The depth of the swim, is it shallow, deep, even or varied? The type of flow, is it slow, medium or heavy, smooth or turbulent? The range at which you need to fish? These are the questions you must ask yourself when you survey your swim. Then, by applying the following rules you can decide which type of float to use.

The most important deciding factor is the direction of the wind. If the wind is upstream, you can fish with a float connected top and bottom. For flowing water this is the best way of fishing. You can control the speed at which the bait travels through the water by holding back on the float and slowing it down, or you can let the bait go through with the speed of the current, checking the float occasionally to ensure that the bait is moving through the water ahead of the float.

If the wind is downstream or across and into your face, it is not possible to do this. The tackle will be uncontrollable due to the wind blowing a bow in your line, which in turn will pull your tackle off course and in towards the bank. In this case a float that is fixed on the line by the bottom end only must be chosen.

First of all let us look at the floats that are fished top and bottom. What materials are they made of, and why? The most popular and commonly used float for trotting is the stick float. Unfortunately many of the stick floats you will see for sale in the shops are of no use for fishing in the way the stick float was designed for — to present the bait at the speed the fish want, and to indicate a bite from the moment the tackle hits the water, to when the float is fully cocked. To achieve this the float is made of cane and balsa of the correct density and in the correct proportions to each other. A correctly made stick float pivots from a point approximately 10 mm below the float tip and it is this pivoting action that makes the float work (see Fig. 33A). At no time is there more than 5 mm of float sticking up above the surface. If a fish intercepts the bait as it is falling through the water the bite is registered immediately by the float tip disappearing below the surface.

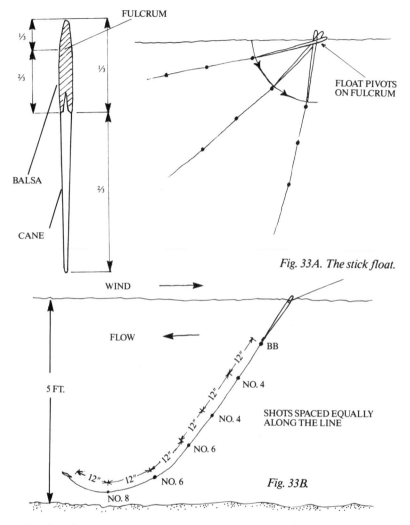

Fig. 33A. The stick float.

Fig. 33B.

The float is connected to the line top and bottom by two pieces of rubber or silicone tube to enable a quick change of the float to one of a different size. The rubbers should be positioned as near to the ends of the float as possible. The type of swim in which a stick float is used should be no more than 8 ft deep and should have a smooth and even flow.

The deeper and heavier the swim the larger the float and shots should be, but always use the lightest float that conditions will allow.

The shots should be evenly spaced out along the line between the float and the hook, with the smallest shots near the hook. Never put a larger shot below a smaller one as this will cause a lot of tangles.

Let us imagine a typical stick float swim. It is 5ft deep with a smooth medium flow. You select a stick float that will take 3 B.B. shot. As previously explained, this is the total approximate shot carrying capacity. You split this up as follows with the shots at 1ft intervals (see Fig. 33B). Set the float at 6 ft so you will be fishing over depth and holding back. At approximately 12″ from the hook we put a No. 8 shot then at 12″ intervals you put on 2 No. 6 followed by 2 No. 4's with a B.B. placed immediately under the float. The object of the B.B. under the float is to give you more weight for casting and to give the float more stability in the water. If you move the float up to give you more depth the shot must be moved up with it and the other shots moved up slightly to keep the spacing even.

When you cast in the tackle you must use a smooth underhand cast, otherwise you will get tangles. To cast the tackle, hold the bait in your left hand (assuming you are right handed) with the rod pointing downwards and then swing the tackle out with a smooth upwards movement. The tackle should land in the water in a nice straight line, ready to indicate a bite. Lift the line off the water and hold back the float to allow the bait to sink in an arc through the water, downstream of the float. The bait must move ahead of the float or the tackle will not function properly and bites will not be indicated.

When the bait has settled, you then smoothly feed off the line from the reel, being very careful not to jerk the float. Every 4 or 5 ft or so hold the line back, checking the float. This causes the bait to rise up in the water, a movement that fish find very attractive and many bites can be induced in this way.

This shotting pattern is standard to all stick floats. The shot sizes are varied to suit the strength of the flow and the depth of the water.

In a shallow swim with a gentle flow, a 3 No. 6 float could be used split into 2 No. 8's and two No. 6's, with the second No. 6 tight up against the float. In a deep heavy moving swim the shots would have to be bigger to get the bait down to the fish, using a No. 4 near the hook and spacing B.B's along the line. The important thing is to obtain a set of stick floats that will do the job they were designed for. Avoid floats with a ring in the base, or floats that feel light. A good stick float has a heavy feel to the stem. Try to buy floats with the name of well known anglers on them. These are usually made of the right materials, otherwise the top names wouldn't recommend them.

A good alternative float to the cane and balsa stick float is the wire stem float. Provided the balance of wire to balsa is in the correct proportion, these floats are a good buy, especially if you are dubious as to the quality of the stick floats that are on sale in your local tackle dealers. Also, due to the stem being so thin they seem to ride better in water that is a bit on the turbulent side with 'boils' or 'swirls' as opposed to a nice smooth glide. I carry a full set of both types with me and I can cope with most conditions with these floats. The shotting patterns are the same as for the cane and balsa sticks.

Whilst the stick float is unbeatable for most flowing water work, it does have its limitations. Its biggest limitation apart from wind direction, is range. To use a stick float properly you have to have a tight line to the float at all times.

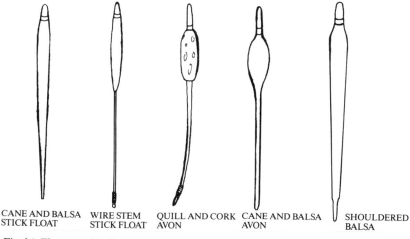

| CANE AND BALSA STICK FLOAT | WIRE STEM STICK FLOAT | QUILL AND CORK AVON | CANE AND BALSA AVON | SHOULDERED BALSA |

Fig. 34. Floats used in flowing water.

Obviously, if the line you want to fish is further than a couple of rod lengths out, a stick float is out of the question. As soon as you tighten on to it, to check it and hold it back, it will move across the river towards you unless you have a very strong upstream wind to hold your line out. In this case you need to let the bait go through the swim at the speed of the current. To do this another type of float is needed. It's called an Avon. This float is made from either a cane stem with a balsa body, or a crowquill stem with a cork body. The latter being the materials first used in the construction of this float. But for modern production methods these materials have been replaced by the cane and balsa. Of the two I prefer the cork on quill and as I make my own floats I have the time to match up the two materials to suit. But crow quills vary in thickness and for mass production the more uniform diameter of cane is favoured.

Do not confuse the Avon float with those hideous fat bodied cumbersome perch bobs that I have told you to avoid. The body of the Avon should be slim and neat. Avoid any so called Avon that has a cork body on a cane stem with fluorescent paint covering half the body as well as the tip. A good Avon has only 12 mm of colour on the tip at the most, and a neat body in proportion to the length of the float. The body should be approximately ¼ - ⅓ of the total length of the float positioned around the upper ⅓ of the stem (see Fig. 34). It is the body that provides most of the floats buoyancy, particularly with the cane and balsa pattern.

The float is shotted so that the body of the float is completely under the surface and only 10 mm of tip is showing. If the wind is strong and causing waves on the surface, it may be necessary to have more of the float tip showing. But always shot a float as far down as conditions will allow.

An Avon float is normally used with the bait just off or just tripping the bottom, so accurate plumbing of the depth is essential. If the bottom is even with little weed growth or few snags, it is also possible to slow the bait down by dragging a foot or so of line along the bottom. But generally speaking an Avon is fished running through with the speed of the flow, with just an occasional check to mend the bow in the line and to lift the tail of the tackle up in the water, as we did with the stick float, to encourage a fish to take the bait.

Notice the difference in the shotting pattern of the Avon to that of the stick (see Fig. 35). The idea is to get the bait down to the fish as soon as possible. I have shown 3 patterns of shotting for light, moderate and heavy flowing waters. Sometimes when fishing you will need to fish a heavier pattern if you intend to fish the far bank. This is because the line which is laying on the surface in the centre of the river will try and overtake the float which is moving at a slower rate. To keep the line behind the float you have to roll the rod tip in an upstream direction to flick the line back up and behind the float. This is called 'mending' the line. You may have to go through this motion half a dozen times over the duration of the trot down your swim. If too light a float is used, every time you mend the line or every time the current pulls the line into a bow, the float will be pulled further and further off its line towards the centre of the

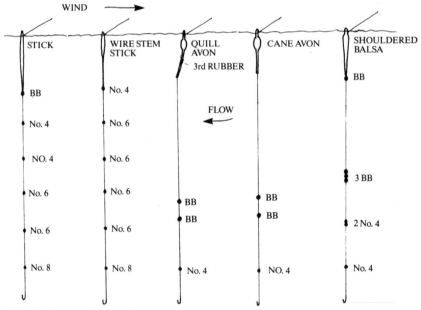

Fig. 35. Basic shotting patterns.

river, so a heavier float is needed to give you something to 'hang' on to when you mend the line and to keep its position near that far shelf for the duration of the trot.

Sometimes it will be a gap between two weed beds that you may want to trot through, and it's no good if the float you are using is too light to hold position. So don't be afraid to go heavier if you need to. If you can't put the bait where the fish are, you won't get a bite anyway, so whenever you need more lead to do the job, don't be frightened to put it on. As long as it is in the right place, it will not deter the fish from taking your bait.

If when fishing you find that the bait has been sucked or taken by a fish and no indication was registered on the float, move your indicating shot down the line closer to the hook. This rule applies no matter which type of float you use, in still or flowing water. The shotting patterns shown in (Fig. 36) are just a guide and can be stepped up or down to suit your own individual floats and waters. You will see also that I have given an alternative pattern for fishing big baits in fast, shallow water, but the general rule is the deeper and faster the water, the heavier the shots.

The Avon floats are fitted to the line just the same as the stick floats but with 3 pieces of tubing if using a quill stemmed float. This is to prevent the lower stem being doubled up and broken on the strike. The third rubber is positioned halfway up the lower stem (see Fig. 35). Most shop bought floats have rings whipped onto the bottom, but ignore these, otherwise you will have to strip your tackle right down to change your float.

Fig. 36

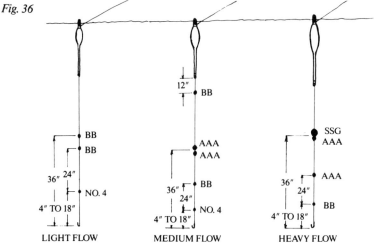

LIGHT FLOW   MEDIUM FLOW   HEAVY FLOW

The other type of float I recommend for use on flowing water in upstream wind conditions is the shouldered balsa. This float is used in fairly deep heavy flowing waters. Being of all balsa construction, they carry a lot of shot for their length. A piece of cane is inserted into the base of the float. This has nothing to do with the operation of the float, it is just to strengthen the base. A thin piece of balsa would probably snap either on the strike or whilst fitting the rubber over it. The shape is also very important. The shoulder is to help prevent the float from riding up too far out of the water when fished holding back. In fact this float can be described as a cross between a stick float and an Avon.

It will not function as well as a stick float in respect of showing a drop bite,

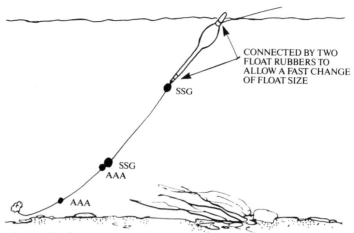

CONNECTED BY TWO
FLOAT RUBBERS TO
ALLOW A FAST CHANGE
OF FLOAT SIZE

SSG

SSG
AAA

AAA

Fig. 37. Avon rig for fishing a large bait in fast shallow water.

but its streamlined shape allows it to be used held back like a stick float with the shots strung out. Stick floats over 5 B.B. capacity are too large and cumbersome to use effectively. A shouldered balsa of the same length and thickness as a 5 B.B. stick float, will carry about 5 A.A.A. shot. Twice the shot load — an important factor when fishing deep heavy water.

Being so buoyant it can also be used with the Avon shotting pattern and run through at the speed of the current. It's a very versatile piece of equipment. But remember it is only used in conditions where heavy shotting is a must. It is no substitute for the stick or the Avon fished properly in the right conditions. As with the other floats it is connected to the line with float tubing.

In certain conditions where the fish will only take a bait slowed right down and the use of the stick float seems essential, but the wind is down stream or in your face, it is sometimes possible to put a double rubber float through satisfactorily by placing a back shot up to 12″ above the float, sinking the line below the surface away from the wind. When using this method, the distance you can fish out from the bank is limited and with the line being beneath the surface, the effectiveness of the strike is less due to the lift of the line being cushioned by the water.

How then do we fish a river in downstream wind conditions? This brings us to the range of floats known as the wagglers. These floats are used with the line connected to the bottom end only to allow you to keep the line under the surface away from the wind. In this way you can fish well out into the river without the float being pulled off line as would happen to a double rubber float in downstream wind conditions. This method can also be used in upstream wind conditions when long range is important and the fish will accept the bait presented in this manner. In waters with a very light flow such as the Fen drains, this is the traditional way to fish with a float, no matter which way the wind is blowing.

They are made of either straight peacock or peacock with balsa bodies. Some of the floats discussed earlier in the still water chapter are ideal for this type of fishing. These would be the larger ones, mainly those without the fine inserts. Fine tips can be a handicap when fishing bottom only in running water. The method is usually used with a small shot or the hook length dragging on the bottom, provided the bottom is snag free (see Fig. 39). So you need a thick buoyant tip to counteract the drag without it going under. The only occasion where a float with a less buoyant insert would be used is in waters with a very light flow, where the fish will have more time to take the bait and may just hold the bait up. In this case a finer insert will register a lift bite better than a thick top.

The wagglers with the balsa bodies are normally used for long range fishing in deep slow moving waters. The reason you sometimes need such a large float with as much as 2 swan shots locking the float is to give enough weight to cast the distance required.

Fig. 38.
Wagglers.

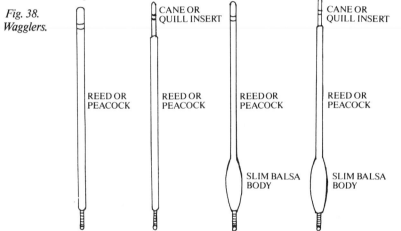

CANE OR
QUILL INSERT

CANE OR
QUILL INSERT

REED OR
PEACOCK

REED OR
PEACOCK

REED OR
PEACOCK

REED OR
PEACOCK

SLIM BALSA
BODY

SLIM BALSA
BODY

When using heavy floats like this it is important to use a heavier main line of about 3½ lbs. These floats have a habit of breaking your line when you cast or strike if fine lines are used. You can still use a fine hook length when fishing with small hooks.

On faster flowing waters it sometimes becomes necessary to slow down the bait. This is done by dragging a small shot along the bottom. In this case we may have as much as 1″ of float tip showing above the surface. The tip will move slowly up and down as the tackle goes through the swim. This movement is caused by the small shot bumping and dragging along the bottom. As soon as the bait is intercepted by a fish, the float will sharply disappear under the surface. After a bit of practice it is quite easy to distinguish between when the bait catches on a snag or when you have a bite. When fishing in a fairly shallow swim, a slow fall of the bait is often the most attractive way of presenting the bait to the fish. In this case, only a couple of light shots will be needed down the line. The deeper the water and the faster the flow, the bigger the float and the shots.

Fig. 39. Shotting patterns for Wagglers.

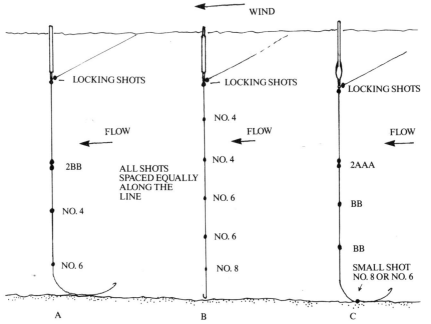

This is the general rule for all types of float fishing. But there is another rule that is the most important of all. ALWAYS, BEFORE FISHING, PLUMB THE DEPTH. The reason for this is twofold. Firstly it is to set the bait accurately to the position on or near the bottom that you want the bait to be. Secondly it allows you to 'see' under the surface to find out the geography of the swim, to see if there are any shelves or holes that are likely places to hold fish. This is done by plumbing various parts of the swim in both a sideways and outwards direction.

Plummets come in two main types. The old traditional cone shaped plummet with a cork insert, into which you place the hook, or the French plummet, which is a clip on type. I prefer the latter, because sometimes it's not just the position of the hook to the float that is important, but the position of the indicating shot to the float that is critical. The clip on plummet has a hollow cut out in the jaws to allow it to clip around a shot in the fully closed position (see Fig. 41). A good alternative to the plummets, particularly on still water, is simply a S.S.G. or A.A.A. shot squeezed onto the hook or line. This has the advantage of being lighter and entering the water with less disturbance. But for flowing water a proper plummet must be used so that it holds bottom against the flow, allowing you to set the float accurately.

Fig. 40. Plumbing the depth.

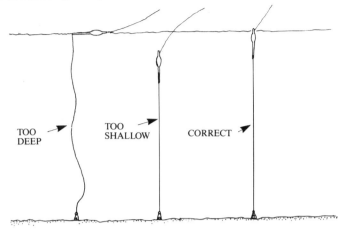

How then do you use a plummet? First of all you set the float to the approximate depth you think the swim is. You then attach the plummet to the shot or hook and cast out with a smooth underhand cast. When the plummet hits the water, leave the bail arm of the reel in the 'off' position to allow the line to be slack. If the float just lies flat or at half cock in the water, it means your tackle is set too deeply, so you must start moving the float back down the line towards the hook. If the float just disappears it means you are not deep enough and you must move the float up the line. When you have got the float set at the correct depth the float will be set so that the tip of the float just sticks up above the surface. You now know that your hook or shot is just on the bottom (Fig. 40).

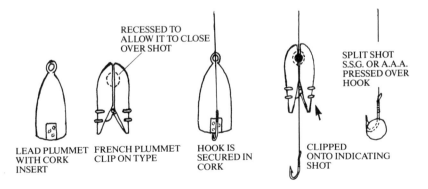

Fig. 41. Types of plummet.

If you want to fish just off the bottom, all you have to do is move the float an inch down the line. If you want to fish on the bottom, you must move the float up the line. But by no more than the amount of line you want lying on the bottom. For example, if your indicating shot is about 18″ above the hook and you move the float up 12″ you know that the indicating shot will be 6″ off the bottom and you have 12″ of hook length laying on the bottom.

Except when you need the indicating shot on the bottom to counteract any drag, explained in the chapter on still water floats, you should always fish with this shot off the bottom, otherwise it will not register a bite properly. Plumbing the depth is normally done before you finish shotting the float. In other words only the two locking shots around the float should be on the line whilst plumbing, then you can accurately shot up the float with regard to the exact depth and the prevailing conditions. As I have said earlier, this process is the key to successful angling.

10 LEGERING METHODS

When I started fishing, legering was a crude, chuck and chance method of fishing, using the rod tip or a dough bobbin as an indicator. A coffin or spiral lead would be slid directly on to the line, stopped with a shot about 18″ from the hook and then thrown in, hoping that a big fish would impale itself on the end. I remember when as a lad, I went night fishing for carp on the Leicester canal. I would leger cheese using the above method across the far side of the canal, laying my rod along the tow path and balancing a halfpenny or a penny if I could afford it on the tip of the rod, with a biscuit or oxo tin placed on the bank underneath the tip. A bite would be signalled by the coin being knocked off the end of the rod and landing in the tin with a loud clatter. You would then strike hoping that the fish was still on the end. It may sound crude, but many a fish was taken using this method. Even so, legering was frowned upon by most anglers, and was only used as a last resort in extreme conditions where float fishing proved to be impossible.

Now, with the tremendous changes we have seen in the past 20 years or so in both bite indication and rod development, legering is an accepted and very important part of the coarse fishing scene. In the mid 1950's when the late Dick Walker said that a National Championship match would be won with leger tactics, everyone laughed and thought he was an idiot. Now in the last 20 years more Nationals have been won with the leger or the bomb as we call it, than with the float. The main reason for this is that the match has been held on mainly bream waters that respond better to leger tactics if a big weight is to be caught than to float fishing methods. This is because they are mainly wide and deep, and the range at which they have to fish, and the fact that the waters are very exposed and have severe wind problems, makes legering tactics far superior to float fishing in terms of both bait presentation and speed. A legered bait can be cast out and got down to the fish far more quickly than with a float fished bait, and with modern bite indicators being as sensitive as they are, bites can be detected easily and in some cases can be induced by the very nature of the direct contact the leger angler has with his terminal tackle.

The big step forward in legering methods was due to the invention of the swing tip by Boston angler Jack Clayton. Although this type of indicator has now fallen out of favour in some areas in preference to later types of indicator, it is still on its day the best method of legering on still waters.

The other big step forward was the development by Dick Walker of the Arlesey bomb. This gave anglers the ability to cast much greater distances and at the same time eliminate most of the tangle problems that were caused by trying to cast less streamlined weights at long range. This is by far the best type of leger weight to use in still water fishing (see Fig. 42). The Arlesey bomb is a streamlined pear shaped lead with a swivel on the top end. This lead is seldom fixed directly onto the main line. It is normally fixed on a link or paternoster, which is fixed to the line either by a ring or a knot (see Fig. 44). The length of the link can be varied depending on the conditions, as can the length of the tail. The tail is the length of line below the link onto which the hook is tied. This length is always of a lesser breaking strain than the main line.

When fishing for bream or roach in open stretches of water, where there are very few weeds or snags, a 2½-3 lb main line with a 1½-2 lb tail is the general set up. If you are fishing for powerful fish like carp, tench or chub, or fishing in snaggy weedy areas, then a much stronger set up used in conjunction with a larger hook is called for. Refer to the chart in the previous chapter on line and hooks for the recommended guide of line strength and tail strength to hook size. This applies whether you are float fishing or legering.

Fig. 42. Types of leger weights.

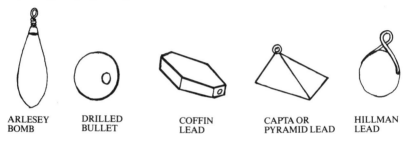

| ARLESEY BOMB | DRILLED BULLET | COFFIN LEAD | CAPTA OR PYRAMID LEAD | HILLMAN LEAD |

Before I go on to describe bite indicators and types of terminal tackle more fully, let's have a look at the rods.

The type of rod to use when legering cannot be tied down to just one rod. It depends on the size and species of fish you are aiming to catch and the types of waters available to you in your area.

If most of your fishing is to be done in rivers like the Hampshire Avon, the Severn or the North Yorkshire rivers like the Ouse and Swale, all of which have a heavy powerful flow, then the species of fish you will be after will be powerful fish like chub and barbel. To handle such fish in these fast waters requires a strong rod between 10-11 ft capable of handling 6-8 lb B.S. lines.

If you are one of the majority who will be fishing for bream and roach on still waters, or slow moving rivers like the Nene, Welland and Witham, then a rod between 9-10 ft with a softer action will be needed. Again ask the advice of your local dealer, telling him what waters you are going to fish. He will then have a good idea which type of rod will suit you the best.

No matter which type of bite indicator you use, before it can indicate you must first of all get a fish to take your bait. The best way to learn to read your tips, is to go to a water that has a large head of willing fish and practice.

It does not matter whether the fish are large or small. The important thing is to get confidence in the method. This can only be done by getting bites and learning to hit them.

When you first start legering you will miss far more bites than you will hit. But the more you practice the better you will become. Sometimes you will get bites that are not bites at all. These are caused by fish swimming along and catching the submerged line, an occurrence that you do not come up against when float fishing. These are called line bites.

They are normally fast sudden jerks of the indicator as opposed to a slow gentle pull. Only practice will teach you to distinguish one from the other.

The Swing Tip

The swing tip is normally a 8-10″ piece of cane connected to a screw fitting with a piece of silicone or rubber tube called a link. Onto the cane is whipped a couple of rings, one at the tip and one ⅔ up towards the link. The link is connected to the rod by the screw, which screws on to a special type of rod tip ring that is a standard fitting on all leger rods (see Fig. 43).

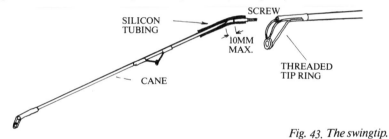

Fig. 43. The swingtip.

For still water, the link is best made of soft silicone tubing. This tubing is sold in long lengths by all good tackle shops. You cut it up to suit yourself for use as swing tip links or as float rubbers. Never have more than 10 mm of loose rubber between the end of the cane and the screw, otherwise the tip will tend to turn over on itself and tangle around your rod tip.

Fig. 44. Types of terminal tackle.

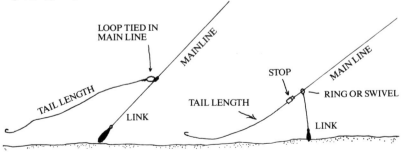

FIXED PATERNOSTER   SLIDING LINK

Terminal Tackle

As I have already shown you in (Fig. 44) there are basically two types of terminal tackle used in legering on still or moderate waters — the sliding link, which uses a bead or other form of stop, and the paternoster where a loop is made in the line and the tail is then tied onto this loop.

Of the two I recommend the paternoster as being the most efficient. It is neater and is less prone to tangles, snags and getting clogged with weed. Beads and leger stops are renowned for picking up floating debris which causes them to jam, so defeating the object of them sliding as they are designed to do. The only time I can see the advantage of them is when the fish are likely to move some distance with the bait before you intend or are able to strike, such as when you are dead bait fishing for pike, zander and eels, or when fishing for

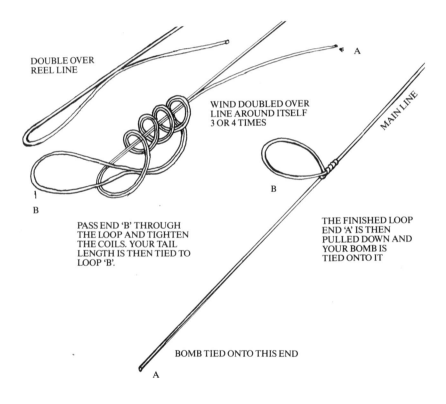

DOUBLE OVER
REEL LINE

WIND DOUBLED OVER
LINE AROUND ITSELF
3 OR 4 TIMES

MAIN LINE

A

B

B

PASS END 'B' THROUGH
THE LOOP AND TIGHTEN
THE COILS. YOUR TAIL
LENGTH IS THEN TIED TO
LOOP 'B'.

THE FINISHED LOOP
END 'A' IS THEN
PULLED DOWN AND
YOUR BOMB IS
TIED ONTO IT

BOMB TIED ONTO THIS END

A

Fig. 45. Tying a paternoster loop.

carp. On these occasions you are not using a rod tip bite indicator. For this type of fishing you use electronic bite alarms and butt indicators, methods I shall cover in my chapter on fishing for big fish.

To make the loop in the line for a paternoster, use the knot shown in (Fig. 45). The reel line is doubled over and then wrapped around itself about 3-4 times. The end is pushed through the loop so that about 12 mm protrudes. Then, by pulling from the other end you tighten up the coils trapping the line so that a loop is left, onto this you tie your tail line. The length of line remaining is trimmed to the length that you want your link to be, and your bomb is then tied onto the end. The length of the tail and link is governed by the way the fish are feeding or by the presentation of the bait that you require.

When fishing for bream or roach in still water, especially in the warmer months, you can expect the fish to be feeding 'off' as well as 'on' the bottom. A slowly falling bait can be more attractive to these fish than a bait just lying on the bottom.

In this case, a tail as long as 6 ft may be used to obtain this falling effect. This would be used in conjunction with a link of about 12″ long (see Fig. 46).

If whilst using this rig you find that the bait is being sucked or taken by the fish and you are not seeing any indication on the tip, then you must shorten the length of the tail to 3-4 ft in the hope of the bite registering properly on the tip.

When you are fishing on the drop like this, it is important that your line is tightened up to the bomb at all times, otherwise a bite will not register. When the bomb hits the bottom, the reel line goes slack. This is the critical moment. You must take the slack out of the line but at the same time see any bites that may occur. Although the bomb has hit the river bed the tail will still be slowly falling through the water and it's at this time you are likely to get a bite.

The way to do it is this; you over cast the baited area by several yards. As soon as the bomb hits the surface of the water, engage the pickup and put the rod onto the rod rests. As the bomb falls through the water it will be drawn towards you in an arc before hitting the baited area. Whilst it is falling it will pull your tip out straight (see Fig. 46A). As it hits the river bed, the tip will collapse. It is at this point you must start taking in slack line, but at the same time you must be looking out for bites.

This is achieved by gently and smoothly winding in the slack line, at the same time trying to keep the tip at the same angle (see Fig. 46B). With a bit of practice you will do this. If the tip rises you will know by the feel whether it is because all the slack has been taken up or because a fish has intercepted the bait. If the tip rises sharply whilst you are winding in gently, it must be a bite, so strike.

If a bite doesn't show on the drop and you know your bait is now lying on the bottom, you must now lift the rod gently and move the bomb a few feet towards you. This is to straighten out the tail. It will probably have fallen in a heap with the line coiled or snaked. You must straighten this so that if a fish picks up the bait the tip will move immediately (Fig. 46C).

If after several minutes the bait still has not been taken, you gently lift the bomb again which in turn lifts the tail, causing the bait to rise up in the water and then to slowly settle again. Continue to do this every few minutes until you know the bait has been pulled through the baited area. You can then wind in and recast. Very often it is as the bait is settling again after a lift that a fish sees it, takes it, and a bite is registered (Fig. 46D).

In the colder months, when water temperatures are very low, the fish will not be moving around in the water as freely as they do when the water is warm. Bites if you can get them will be very shy, so the length of tail is kept down to 2-3 ft in length. The link is reduced to about 9″ in still water and to 6″ in flowing water. Also the bait is left much longer between lifts, as continual casting across the water will unsettle the fish and make them even more reluctant to feed.

When you set up your rod rests for swing tipping you will need three rests to support your rod properly. Avoid rod rests with fork tops and thin stems. The best rod rests are the wide type with polythene tubing stretched across the top (see Fig. 46). These are bought separately from the bank sticks into which they screw. A good bank stick is made of aluminium tube of at least 12 mm dia. with a brass insert on the end, into which the rod rest head is screwed. The all in one type of rod rests with the V tops and thin stems are useless. They spin round or collapse causing your rods to fall into the water, or your line snags on the edges causing it to snap when you strike. This loses tackle and fish, both of which are valuable. Never have more than 12″ of rod tip hanging over the end of the rod rest when legering, otherwise you will lose the sensitivity of the tip due to it bouncing about in the wind. Position the rod pointing downstream if the water has a slight flow, at an angle of 90°-120° to the line (see Fig. 48) this is the most effective angle when striking to set the hook home. When you tighten your line to the bomb your swing tip should be set just off the vertical (see Fig. 46C). This is so that if a fish swims towards you with the bait, the tip will fall back, indicating that the bomb has been moved. If this happens strike.

The swing tip should also be positioned just above the surface of the water, if possible. Sometimes because of marginal weed growth you need to have it higher, so that the line is clear of the weeds when it enters the water. If possible, providing the water is not deep or the shelf is not too steep, it pays to wade out and clear a channel through the weed so that your line can lie unhindered in the water. To do this you fit a weed cutter attachment to your landing net handle. Always take care whenever you start to wade for any reason. Test the river bed in front of you with the aid of your landing net handle. Make sure it does not drop away suddenly and that the bottom is firm. If you have any doubts do not wade.

Some rivers like the Witham and the Nene and some of the Fen drains are run off as the tide turns. This run off is controlled by large sluice gates being opened and closed. This means that the river can be still when you start fishing and then suddenly start moving slowly. Sometimes if a surplus of water is allowed into the river but the main sluice is closed, the river can even back up and go the 'wrong' way. These movements are indicated by the swing tip being drawn out and not settling back as normal. Wind and undertow can also cause

Fig. 46.

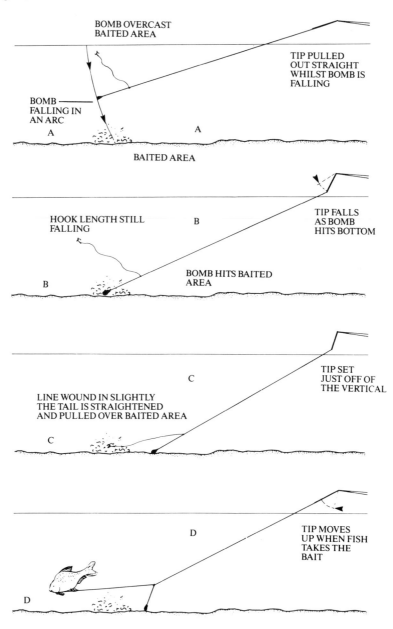

BOMB OVERCAST
BAITED AREA

TIP PULLED
OUT STRAIGHT
WHILST BOMB IS
FALLING

BOMB
FALLING IN
AN ARC

A

A

BAITED AREA

HOOK LENGTH STILL
FALLING

B

TIP FALLS
AS BOMB
HITS BOTTOM

BOMB HITS BAITED
AREA

B

C

TIP SET
JUST OFF OF
THE VERTICAL

LINE WOUND IN SLIGHTLY
THE TAIL IS STRAIGHTENED
AND PULLED OVER BAITED AREA

C

D

TIP MOVES
UP WHEN FISH
TAKES THE
BAIT

D

Fig. 47. Swingtip Rod. Seat box can be used to support rod butt whilst legering.

this. In these circumstances you need to do one of two things, either weight the tip with lead wire to act against the pull, or fit a moulded rubber link in place of the silicone rubber tube (see Fig. 49). You also need to do this in very windy weather to stop the tip being blown about, otherwise it becomes very difficult to pick out the movements that show you have a bite.

Of the two methods, I prefer to use the moulded rubber link. It is very effective and many of the top match anglers have adopted its use in preference to the old method of weighting the tip with lead wire.

These links can be bought separately from the tips in packets of 3 or 4, each link being of a different strength. Naturally you always use the 'weakest' one that conditions allow. The strongest of the set will cope with quite a good strength of flow before straightening out, but I would normally switch to another form of indication in preference to using a really strong swing tip link. This is because a very strong link can affect both the range and accuracy of the cast to a certain degree.

Sometimes, when we are swing tipping in still water, either due to being on a high bank, or because of the depth of the water, the angle of the line coming out of the water to the swing tip is too shallow to make bite indication possible (see Fig. 50).

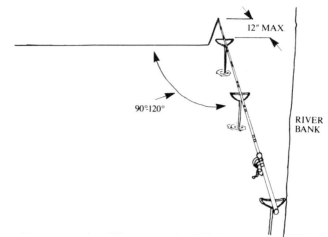

Fig. 48. Correct position of rod when swingtipping.

In these circumstances either a long parallel quiver tip or a spring tip can be used. In still or slow flowing water under these conditions, the spring tip is by far the more sensitive. Due to the hinge action produced by the spring being at the bottom of the indicator, there is no progressive resistance for a taking fish to feel. Bites are positive and hittable. Several sizes of spring tip can be used, the size being classified by the length of the tip and the strength of the spring, the two factors that determine the sensitivity of the tip.

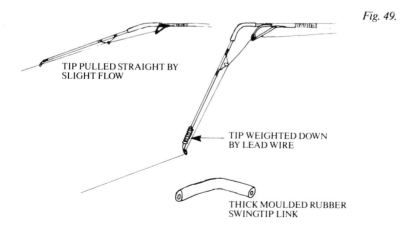

Fig. 49.

TIP PULLED STRAIGHT BY SLIGHT FLOW

TIP WEIGHTED DOWN BY LEAD WIRE

THICK MOULDED RUBBER SWINGTIP LINK

The best form of indication on flowing water is the quiver tip. These are made from pieces of tapered or parallel fibreglass that screw into the end of your leger rod. The difference between the parallel and the tapered tips is the way the tips bend (see Fig. 53). The parallel tips bend from the lower part of the tip and act like a hinge. These are far more sensitive than the tapered tips but are limited by the strength of the flow. Anything more than a moderate flow and they bend over too far and will not indicate a bite. But for slow flowing waters they are superior to the tapered tip.

The taper tip gives a progressive resistance as it bends. The further it bends, the more the resistance of the tip. If used with a rod with a soft top joint in strong flowing water, the top section will move with the quiver tip so making it ineffective (see Fig. 52A). A stiffer rod top is needed when quiver tipping in strong flowing water. In fact the best type of rod for these conditions is one which has the quiver tip spliced into the rod top forming part of the rod itself. In this way a nice progression of taper is achieved.

Ideally, only a slight curve is wanted on the quiver tip to allow the bite to indicate properly. The rod tip must be well supported to stop it bending with the tip and to stabilize it in windy conditions. Excessive overhang of the rod tip will make bite indication very difficult to spot. One way of easily spotting very shy bites and protecting the tip from the worst effects of wind, is to use a target board. These can be made from Formica or thin perspex, but do not fall into the trap of making them too gaudy. They are best painted matt black with lines of a dull colour to give enough contrast, without dazzling you or giving you eyestrain. (see Fig. 52).

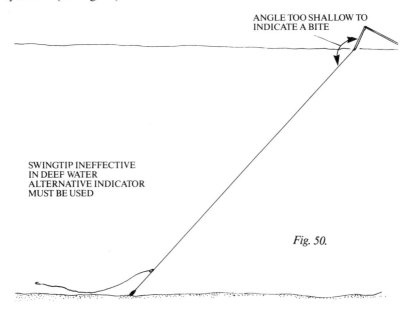

ANGLE TOO SHALLOW TO
INDICATE A BITE

SWINGTIP INEFFECTIVE
IN DEEP WATER
ALTERNATIVE INDICATOR
MUST BE USED

Fig. 50.

Another factor as well as flow that determines how much bend you have in your tip is the weight of your leger. The heavier your lead the more the tip will bend. So it is important that you use the smallest weight you can to hold the position in the river that you want to fish. Also the force of the water against the line has a marked effect on the bend of the tip. If you require a bait to be held well out in strong flowing water, the rod must be held or supported in a near vertical position. This is so that the least amount of line possible is actually in the water (see Fig. 54). When you need to fish with the rod in a horizontal position, lay the rod pointing downstream with the line going off at 90°-120° to the rod tip (see Fig. 55), in this way any bites will be indicated immediately. Sometimes a bite will be indicated by the tip straightening instead of bending further. This means a fish has picked up the bait and is moving towards you or upstream, so strike.

The terminal tackle used in flowing water is basically the same as in still water. The paternoster is still the best set up in most conditions, with the only difference being the lengths of tail and link and in certain conditions the type of leger weight. In flowing water the tail and link is much shorter, 12-18″ is the normal starting length of tail, with a 6-9″ link.

Normally when fishing at close to medium range one or two S.S.G. shot clipped to the link makes a very effective and cheap form of leger weight. If due to the speed of the current you cannot hold the bait where you want it, a coffin lead or a capta lead can be used. When fishing at long range a slightly flattened Arlesey bomb can be used if you need to hold out. Capta leads, although they are very effective at holding the bottom are, due to their shape, awkward to cast any distance without tangling problems.

When a rolling bait is needed to search the river bed in an arc from the centre of the river to the edge, a drilled bullet is the type of leger weight to use. This is slid directly onto the main line and stopped with a split shot to whatever length of tail you require, (see Fig. 51). No link is needed when fishing this method.

Fig. 51.

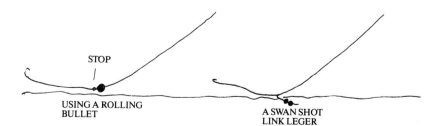

STOP

USING A ROLLING
BULLET

A SWAN SHOT
LINK LEGER

Fig. 52. Correctly supporting the rod whilst quivertipping (inset, using a target board).

Fig. 52A.

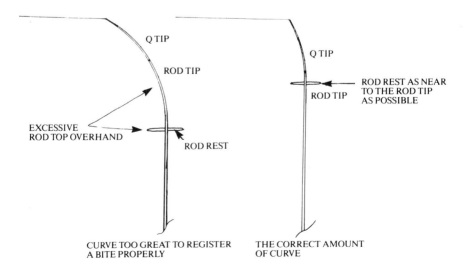

Q TIP

Q TIP

ROD TIP

ROD REST AS NEAR
TO THE ROD TIP
ROD TIP   AS POSSIBLE

EXCESSIVE
ROD TOP OVERHAND

ROD REST

CURVE TOO GREAT TO REGISTER   THE CORRECT AMOUNT
A BITE PROPERLY   OF CURVE

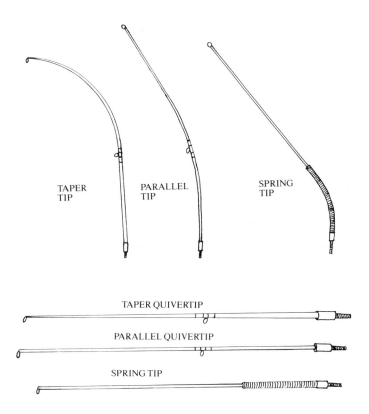

TAPER
TIP

PARALLEL
TIP

SPRING
TIP

TAPER QUIVERTIP

PARALLEL QUIVERTIP

SPRING TIP

Fig. 53. Action of bite indicators.

Swim Feeders

A very popular method of legering that seems to be ever on the increase is the swim-feeder. This method allows you to bait the area immediately around your hook bait and realease your feed in either one lump when using an open end feeder, or in a steady trickle when using the block end type. Accurate casting is a must, if you want to concentrate your feed and the fish in a narrow area of the swim. If care is not taken the bait and the fish will be scattered all across the river or lake and the advantage of using a feeder will be lost. Swim-feeders are best fished using a sliding link. They are quite bulky and heavy and can impair either the indication or the strike unless a sliding link is used. Some swim-feeders are now on the market that are a lot slimmer and lighter than the earlier models, but they are only for using with maggot baits. The large open ended feeders still need to be used for feeding large or still baits like luncheon meat, bread, sweetcorn and casters.

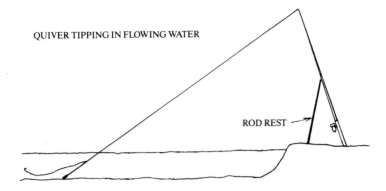

Fig. 54. Holding out in fast flowing water.

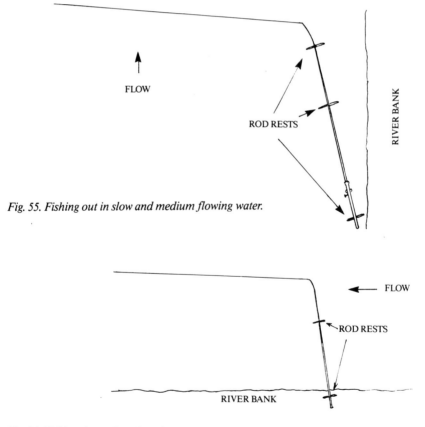

Fig. 55. Fishing out in slow and medium flowing water.

Fig. 56. Fishing down the side in fast water.

To fill an open ended feeder you have to plug the ends with ground bait with samples of your hook bait in the centre. The groundbait must be stiff enough to withstand the entry into the water, but must break up quickly once the feeder is in position on the river bed. Only trial and error can teach you the right mix for your particular waters. Never put ready mixed ground bait into a blockend feeder as it will clog the holes and stop your maggots from wiggling out. If you want to slow down the rate at which the maggots empty themselves from the feeder, use a pinch or two of dry ground bait or bran mixed in with the maggots. Always put your hookbait onto the hook before filling a blockend feeder with maggots, otherwise by the time you have changed your hookbait the feeder will have emptied itself.

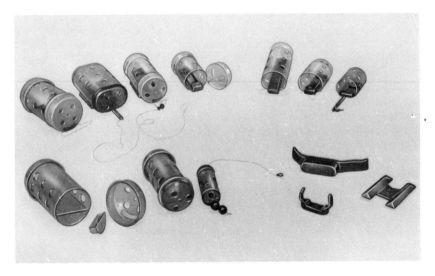

Fig. 57. Swimfeeders and additional leads.

Large blockend feeders with extra strips of lead attached to them are now used regularly on rivers such as the Trent and Severn. Normal light leger rods cannot cast or retrieve these without being overloaded. Specialist tip action feeder rods with test curves of 1 lb plus and built in quivertips have to be used.

Because of the weight of the feeder and the range at which they are fished, the rods are normally positioned upright whilst fishing. (See Fig. 54). 5 lb or 6 lb line must be used to withstand the force needed to cast these heavy rigs, but the hooklengths are still matched to the hook and bait size as recommended in the chapter on line and hooks.

The feeders are best attached to the line with special links that are slightly elasticated to withstand the shock of casting, reducing the risk of the feeder "cracking off" on the cast. The sliding bead is stopped either side with a 3 to 6 inch gap between the stops to act like a bolt rig. (See Fig. 78).

11 THE ROACH POLE

The roach pole has seen a large increase in its popularity and use over the last few years. Not so long ago, most tackle dealers would sell you a roach pole but looked at you gone out if you asked them if they stocked the terminal tackle required to make it perform correctly. As well as being ignorant as to what type of terminal tackle should be used with a roach pole, they showed very little interest in trying to obtain it. It was very much akin to selling someone a car without an engine and then telling them it was impossible to get one.

Fortunately, this situation has changed. Pole specialists, through the angling press have educated the dealer and the manufacturers as to what type of tackle is used with a pole, and most dealers now stock most of the various items that are required.

As with all tackle, the quality varies, not so much in the materials used, but in the design of the tackle, especially the floats.

Many of the floats on sale are classed as pole floats, but they are much bigger and heavier than the types used by the continental match anglers. Others are of the correct size and shape but need modification before they will do the job they are designed for properly. These modifications will be dealt with later on. Before you start buying any pole fishing equipment, you must have a full understanding of how it works and why it is designed the way it is. Pole fishing is split up into two separate methods. One is for taking fish from the surface and midwater areas, and the other method is for bottom fishing, which means you are seeking fish either on or just off the bottom.

Each method uses a different type of pole and terminal tackle and a different approach to the style of fishing and the methods of feeding.

Let us first of all look at the bottom fishing method. The complete rig is shown in Fig. 58. This style of fishing is very different to the normal rod and reel method that British anglers have always used. The object of fishing this way is to present a bait quickly to the fish with both accuracy and finesse. It allows you greater control over the tackle and to use much finer lines and hooks, giving you a much more efficient bait presentation without the worries of being broken up by the fish.

To achieve this you must use the correct type of pole, float and terminal tackle. If this important balance of equipment is not maintained then serious problems will occur.

Firstly the Pole

For bottom fishing a stiff actioned pole of the 'take apart' type is essential. The tip section should also be stiff and onto the end of this an aluminium or fibreglass crook is fitted (see Fig. 58). When buying a new pole it is sometimes

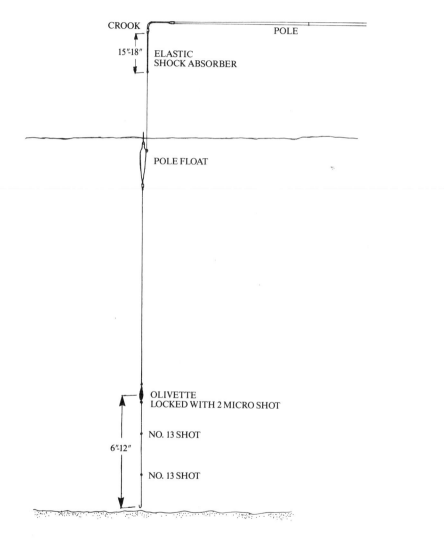

Fig. 58A. Bottom fishing continental style.

necessary to cut off several inches of tip from the end of the top joint before the crook will fit properly. Ask your tackle dealer to do this job for you. The reason for this crook is to be able to fit the length of elastic shock absorber used when fishing this style quickly and securely, at the same time holding the elastic at right angles to the pole to eliminate the tangles that would be caused if the elastic was connected to the end of the pole without the crook. A more efficient method now favoured by most matchmen is to use a conversion kit which is available from most tackle shops. This allows you to run the elastic inside the top joints of the pole.

The kit consists of a number of different sizes of internal or external end fittings, and different sizes of fluted plugs to suit the internal diameters of the various end sections. The smallest will fit into the top section of most poles, and the largest as far down as the 4th section, allowing as much as 6ft of elastic to be used. When using the longer lengths of elastic, the strength is usually made up to give a progressive resistance by having different strengths of elastic joined together, with the finer strength nearest to the tip. (See Fig. 58B).

The plugs have two eyes, one either side. The elastic is tied onto the large eye, and a length of thick line or thin nylon cord is tied onto the small eye at the other end. This is to allow you to pull the plug out of the pole section when you need to remove or change the elastic. Onto the end of the elastic you then connect the line. This can be 1½ lbs B.S. or 1 lb B.S. depending on the breaking strain of our hook length. If a 1 lb B.S. hook length is to be used then a 1½ lb B.S. mainline is needed. If an 8 oz or 12 oz hook length is to be used then a 1 lb B.S. mainline is normally sufficient (see chart).

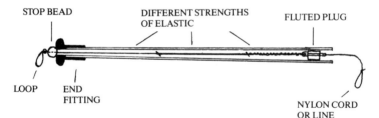

Fig. 58B. Pole top conversion kit.

The length of the main line is determined by the depth of water and the conditions prevailing at the time. The distance from the bank you intend to fish, in addition to the depth of water, will determine the length of pole that is to be used. Obviously the various permutations taking all these things into account are endless. This is why the continentals carry several hundred different types of readily assembled tackles with them when they go fishing. Some anglers will obviously not be able to afford these vast amounts of tackles, so a compromise must be reached and the choice of tackles reduced to an acceptable level without leaving the angler handicapped in any normal situation.

Floats for Bottom Fishing
The choice of the float to be used when pole fishing is reached as when fishing with a rod and reel. It is largely dependent upon the type of water and the prevailing weather conditions. The length of pole to be used also has to be considered in choosing the size of the float. The longer the length of pole to be used, the larger the size of the float. This is to allow you sufficient weight to cast out easily to the required distance.

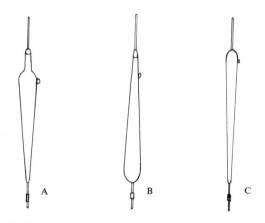

Fig. 59. Pole floats.

If a light float is used with a long pole, especially in windy conditions, it will make casting difficult and only result in tangles. Study the chart of suggested float sizes to pole lengths. Keep to this and no problems should arise. The types of pole floats can be limited to 3 basic types for bottom fishing and a set of 4 or 5 different sizes of each type will be necessary (see Fig. 59). You can start with just one type of float if you intend to use a roach pole on just one type of water. This will keep the number of floats required to just 4 or 5.

Float 'A' is the best pattern of float to use in deep still waters in fairly calm conditions. Float 'B' can be used on still waters in most conditions and is the best type to buy if only one set of floats can be afforded initially. Float 'C' is used in slow moving waters such as drains and canals. All three floats have certain things in common. They are all made of balsa wood, they all have fine bristle tips and most importantly, they all have fine wire eyes at the side of the floats near the top.

All pole floats are connected to the line at the top and bottom. This is so you can control the tackle properly from the pole tip. The float is held in position by a plastic float cap which slides over the bottom stem of the float. The length of fine bristle tip is sensitive to only one No. 13 dust shot, so ultra sensitive shotting is required to set the float in the water so that only the bristle is showing. If silicon or rubber tube was used to connect the line at the top of the float, this would upset this fine balance at the tip due to the surface tension acting on the increased surface area of the rubber. The amount of extra shot needed to pull the rubber clear of the surface tension would exceed the shotting capacity of the float and once the surface tension acting around the rubber was broken the float would then sink, rendering it useless.

To overcome this problem a very fine wire ring made from 5 amp fuse wire is fitted near to the top of the float and the line is then threaded through this. This is the modification sometimes needed to be done to shop bought pole floats, although most of the imported continental made floats are already fitted with this ring (see Fig. 65).

The Olivette

This is the pear shaped lead weight used to form the bulk of the shotting capacity of the float. By concentrating the weight into this fine streamlined lead, casting out the tackle is made an easy tangle free operation and the bait is quickly taken down to the fish. The olivettes are mounted on fine wires and when removed a tiny hole is left through the centre. It is then threaded onto the line and locked into position by placing a No. 10 or No. 12 micro dust shot each side. The thinnest end should be pointing upwards towards the float.

The olivettes come in different sizes and are numbered 1, 2, 3, 4, 5, 6 etc. The lower numbers being the smaller weights. When setting up your tackles, the floats must be matched accurately to the olivettes. Apart from the olivette and its two small locking shots, only two No. 13 micro dust shots are placed below it on the hook length (see Fig. 58). Let us say for example that we want to use a

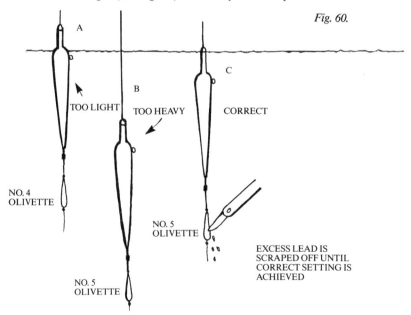

Fig. 60.

A

TOO LIGHT   B   TOO HEAVY   C   CORRECT

NO. 4
OLIVETTE

NO. 5
OLIVETTE

NO. 5
OLIVETTE

EXCESS LEAD IS
SCRAPED OFF UNTIL
CORRECT SETTING IS
ACHIEVED

float which will take a No. 4 or 5 olivette. Looking at the chart on weight sizes to pole lengths you can see that you will use this size when fishing with an 18 ft to 22ft pole.

Using a deep water jug or tank to test them with, you attach the No. 4 olivette to the bottom of the float with a short piece of line. The lead should then be locked onto the line with the same size of small shots you intend to use on the finished tackle. You now place the float and lead into the tank or jug. Let us suppose that the float sits in the water with more length of tip showing above the surface than the two No. 13 shots that will be fixed on to the hook length, will pull down (see Fig. 60A). This means that the bulk shot is too light. So you must now fit on the next size of olivette, which in this case will be a No. 5.

The chances are that this will be too heavy for the float and the float will sink to the bottom of the jug or tank (see Fig. 60B). This is fine. What you now have to do is to take a modelling knife and trim off pieces of lead from the olivette until the float rises to the surface and just a small amount (1 mm) of the balsa tip is showing (see Fig. 60C). The float is now properly trimmed. When the tackle is made up and the two No. 13 shots are fitted onto the hook length, the float will be set to its proper position. If it should sink or ride a little too low in the water an additional light scraping of the olivette will do the trick. If it rides too high, then replace the locking shots around the olivette with one or two shots of a slightly larger size.

Let us now have a look at the completed tackle set up (see Fig. 58). You have the stiff take apart pole onto which is fitted the crook. Onto this the elastic is fitted by a loop being placed into the slot of the crook and held into place with a plastic sheath, or run inside the pole if using a conversion kit. The elastic is either fine, medium or heavy in strength. The strength of the elastic is determined by the size of the fish you are expecting to catch and the size of the hook being used. This balance is very important if you intend to fish effectively.

Pole Length	Float and Olivette Size		
9 ft-12 ft	Size 0 to Size 2		
12 ft-15 ft	Size 2 to Size 4		
18 ft-22 ft	Size 4 to Size 6		
22 ft-27 ft	Size 6 upwards		
Hook Size	**Elastic**	**Main Line**	**Hook Length**
24-22	Fine	1 lb B.S.	8 oz to 12 oz B.S.
20-18	Medium	1-1½ lb B.S.	12 oz to 1 lb B.S.
18-16	Medium to Strong	1½-2 lb B.S.	1 lb to 1½ lb B.S.
16-14	Extra Strong	2 lb-3 lb B.S.	1½ lb to 2½ lb B.S.

Extra strong elastic can be achieved by doubling over the heavy grade of elastic and twisting or plaiting it together. The length of the elastic should be between 15 and 18 inches for maximum efficiency.

The elastic acts as a shock absorber when playing the fish. It will stretch to almost six times its original length, cushioning the fishes initial run and drawing it upwards through the water with a pumping action. Fish can be played out much quicker on a roach pole using elastic than they can with a rod and reel.

The floats as previously explained, are selected to suit the type of water and the size of float is dependent upon the length of pole to be used, along with the recommended size of olivette used with that length of pole. The length of line between the pole top and the float should be kept as short as possible. The ideal way of using the pole is to control the tackle from directly above it. Bites are then connected with a smooth lifting of the pole tip as opposed to the conventional strike.

The length of the pole that you need to use is decided by the distance from the bank that you intend to fish and the depth of the water. The closer the fish can be brought into the bank the shorter the pole you need to use. If fishing alongside the marginal weed of a river or pond then a 15 ft or 18 ft length of pole will probably be sufficient. If you need to fish over the near shelf on rivers such as the Witham or Welland, then you may need a 22 ft or even a 27 ft length to reach this.

Again a large number of permutations of tackle length and size of olivette can soon be built up. But if you work on the principle that the further out you fish the deeper the water is likely to be, then these can be cut down in number by having the smaller sizes of floats on shorter lines and the heavier tackle on longer lines.

The olivettes should be locked onto the line just above the hook length. The hook length is never more than 6 to 12 inches in length. Two No. 13 microdust shot are spaced evenly along the hook length. If the bites are shy, the shots can be moved together closer to the hook to give a more positive indication of a bite.

Several minutes of careful plumbing around the swim is essential for good results. Any holes or shelves should be located and noted and the tackle should be fished over these areas where possible. The float must be set so that the hook is exactly 15 mm to 25 mm off the bottom. This is so that when the fish move into the baited area, the bait on the hook will hit them smack between their eyes and the tackle will register immediately it has been taken by the fish.

Once the area to be fished has been decided upon and the tackle set to the exact depth, a couple of balls of groundbait loaded with feeders can be introduced into the swim. The groundbait should be mixed fairly stiffly so as to start breaking up near to or on the bottom. It is here you are wanting to catch the fish, so you do not want the feed to start breaking up in mid-water and bring the fish up off the bottom.

When a fish is hooked and played on a roach pole, it may be necessary to remove sections to bring the fish in, especially when fishing a long pole in shallow water. This operation must be done smoothly (Fig. 64). The best way to do it is to slide the pole down across your thigh removing the sections as you go. If a small fish has been hooked it will only be necessary to remove enough

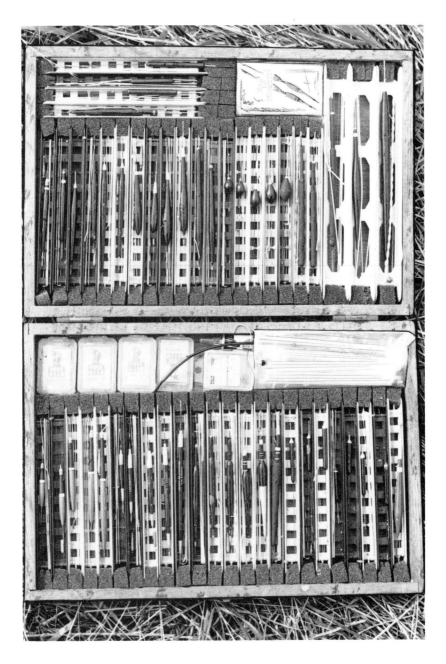

Fig. 61. Pole tackles complete with winders.

Fig. 62. Holding a pole correctly whilst seated.

Fig. 63. Holding a pole correctly whilst standing.

Fig. 64A. Removing sections from a pole to land a fish.

Fig. 64B. Removing sections from a pole whilst seated.

sections to allow the fish to be swung into your hand. If the fish is larger and requires netting, an additional section must be removed to allow the fish to be drawn over the net without lifting it from the water.

Never lift a hooked fish straight up and out of the water. Always bring it sideways away from the baited area before bringing it to the surface, otherwise the disturbance caused by the fish being brought across the surface will frighten the shoal.

When fishing with a long pole, the pole is held across the thigh, holding the pole down with the right hand behind the body and supporting it with the left hand under the pole in front of your knee (see Fig. 62).

If you are fishing from a steep or sloping bank, you may be unable to break down the pole by sliding the sections off and behind you. In these circumstances the pole must be brought around parallel to the bank and across your thigh, and the sections slid off from the side (Fig. 64B).

Never try to hold a long pole under your forearm as you would a rod. It will be totally unmanageable and difficult to hit your bites. This then is the basic method of bottom fishing continental style. Let us now have a look at the method for fishing off the surface and mid-water areas.

The type of pole used for this style of fishing is known as a flick tip pole. The top joint, instead of being rigid as used when bottom fishing, is soft and has a tapered piece of solid fibreglass spliced into the end. The pole itself can be a take-apart with a flick tip type top joint fitted, or can be of the telescopic type.

When buying a pole, a take-apart should be your priority. This type of pole can be used for bottom fishing or midwater and surface fishing. As most of your pole fishing will be bottom fishing then this is the type of pole for you. The telescopic type, although cheaper than the take-apart poles, can only be used for small fish using the flick tip method. They are too soft and floppy to use with a crook and elastic, so money spent on a telescopic pole will be wasted. Also when buying a pole, one shorter than 27 ft should not be considered unless funds are really tight. You will not be able to use a 27 ft pole at its full length straight away, but a take-apart pole can be used at any length from 6 ft upwards by adding or taking away the sections. It only takes a few weeks to get used to handling the longer lengths of pole and if a shorter pole is bought you will then come across the problem of being restricted in length and unable to reach the fish. So avoid shorter poles than 27 ft.

When using a flick tip pole the line is connected to the end of the pole by a short length of line a couple of pounds heavier in breaking strain to the main line. This is because most of the shock and pressure is taken by the line closest to the tip, especially where it is tied onto the small eye normally whipped onto the end of the tip. No elastic shock absorber is used with this method, as it is mainly used for catching small fish like bleak, small roach and small rudd. The floats are also different. They are a lot finer and they take very little shot. A sharp contrast to the heavier type used when bottom fishing.

The type I use are all home made, using small pieces of peacock quill with 24 or 22 gauge piano wire stems. For the really fine ones, the spring wire on which the olivettes are mounted can be used (see Fig. 65). A piece of fine 5 amp fuse wire is wrapped around a needle and the ends twisted together to make the eye. This is then glued into the side of the peacock to make the type of fine ring described earlier (see Fig. 65). The tops of the floats can be left flat or can have a short nylon or wire bristle. This must not be long as used with the bottom floats or the balance of the float will be upset.

The small plastic float caps used to connect the float to the line, are made by cutting the plastic insulation from off the very fine signal wires found inside connecting cables on hi-fi equipment and telephone cables. For fishing with long poles, balsa bodied floats made slightly larger and with heavier wire stems can be used. These are easier to cast than the light peacock ones but are not as sensitive.

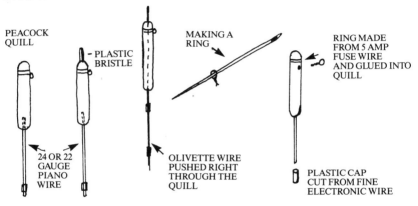

Fig. 65. *Pole floats used for fishing surface and midwater.*

When casting your pole tackle always use a side or under hand cast, casting into the wind, otherwise tangles will occur.

The shotting patterns used vary depending on whereabouts in the water the fish are feeding. A loaded float can be used taking just a couple of No. 13 dust shots if fish are to be caught near the surface. A faster progressive fall can be achieved by using what is known as a logarithmic shotting pattern. This is used when fishing at mid-water in deep water, or when fishing near the bottom in shallow water. A range of shotting patterns is shown in Fig. 66. The length of line between float and pole tip can be short as described in the section on bottom fishing, or if speed fishing for bleak or small rudd and roach, where the bite rate is very fast, the line can be left long enough to allow the fish to be swung into your hand without taking down sections of the pole. When using a telescopic pole, the tackle has to be fished this way due to the difficulty in collapsing the pole. This again amplifies the limitations of the telescopic type of pole as against the versatility of the take-apart pole.

Some poles have a line winding attachment whipped onto the second or third section of the pole below the tip. This can be used whilst using a flick tip, for shortening your length of line whilst fishing and storing the surplus line until you need to lengthen it again. This is very useful if you have a limited number of readily assembled tackles, or if you intend to change your depth or range a number of times during the session.

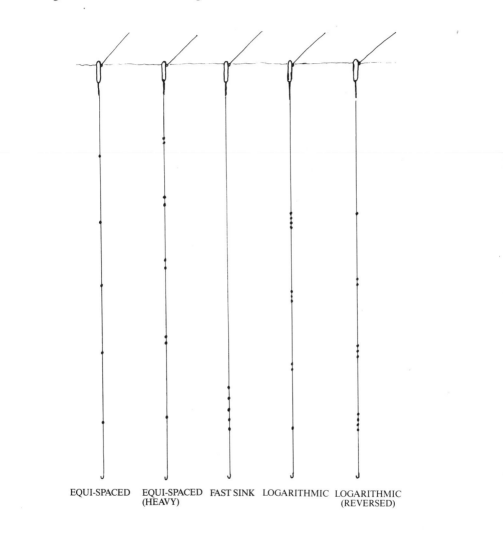

EQUI-SPACED   EQUI-SPACED   FAST SINK   LOGARITHMIC   LOGARITHMIC
               (HEAVY)   (REVERSED)

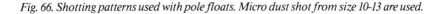

Fig. 66. Shotting patterns used with pole floats. Micro dust shot from size 10-13 are used.

When feeding the swim at surface or midwater levels, the groundbait is mixed very wet or softly and must break up immediately on or near the surface. Feeder maggots can be added to this mix, but it is better if these are loose fed, as they tend to climb out of the mixing bowl when a wet mix is being used.

Because of the fineness of the tackle, most anglers make up their tackles at home and wind them onto plastic winders, using different coloured winders as a code to the different lengths of tackle. To ensure that the winders unwind easily, it is important to wind the tackle on carefully. A centre peg is moulded into each end of the winders and the tackle below the float should be kept to one side of this. Then, when the float has been wound on, you cross over and wind the remaining line and elastic onto the other side. The loop of the elastic is then slipped over the centre peg to hold it securely. When winding on a tackle that does not use the elastic, the end can be held by slipping a piece of float rubber onto the end of the line and then sliding this over the peg.

Different lengths of winders can be bought in differences of 1 cm in length. I normally keep to one size of winder, at 14 cm. This size will hold most of the float sizes I use and can be stored more easily in slotted foam than a lot of different sizes.

12 ADVANCED METHODS AND TACKLE

For fishing under normal conditions the methods and tackle previously described will generally cope. There will be times however, due to excessive depths, restrictive swims, peculiarities in the fishes feeding habits and other abnormal conditions, when specially designed or adapted tackle and methods will be needed.

Some situations you may come up against in your angling career will be unique to a particular water, and you will have to adapt your own methods and ideas to overcome them.

A special float or other item of tackle may need to be made to overcome a particular problem associated with the water or the fish.

The methods described here have already been designed to overcome some of the existing known problems that anglers are likely to come up against. But they are not necessarily at the peak of their development. They are still open to improvement and adaption.

The Sliding Float

Sliding floats are used in conditions of deep water, or where bankside growth or height makes it difficult to cast at fixed depths. Also when pike fishing with a heavy live or dead bait, a sliding float will be needed for any depth over 4 or 5 feet if a long cast is to be achieved easily.

Still water sliders are made with cane or peacock antennas, supported by a balsa body (see Fig. 67A). Normally a very small float ring made by wrapping 15 amp fuse wire around a needle or a pin is used, together with a sliding stop knot. The quick change float attachments made from biro tubes as described in the chapters on float fishing are ideal for sliders. The small pin hole made in the bottom of the tube is ideal for this, with the added advantage that any Antenna or bodied peacock float can be used as a slider. The only disadvantage of using a small hole is that it takes time for the line to be pulled through. It can stick and need to be twitched through, causing a jerky fall of the bait. Also, if a large float is used, the strike can be impaired by the float being pulled through the water.

The solution to this is to use a float with a standard sized ring and fit a small balsa bead with a pin hole through the middle onto the line between the float and the stop knot (see Fig. 67B). This will slide freely up and down the line and the large ring on the float will allow the line to run smoothly and freely, as both the bait and tackle fall through the water and also on the strike.

These beads are easily made by cutting 4 mm long pieces from a length of 5 mm dia. balsa dowel. A pin is pushed through the centre and then the bead is dipped into varnish. When the varnish is dry the pin is removed leaving a small diameter hole (see Fig. 68).

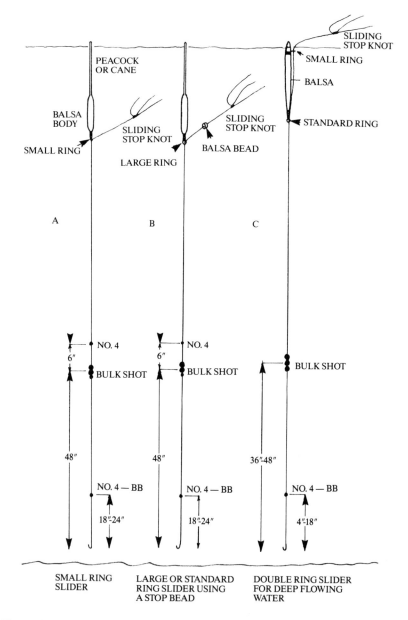

Fig. 67. Sliding Floats.

Floats used for flowing water need two rings. One at the bottom and one just below the tip. The bottom ring can be of the normal diameter, but the top ring needs to be small. Balsa beads cannot be used with these floats.

The floats are normally made from all balsa and shaped like a standard taper stick float, but with a thicker diameter body (see Fig. 67C). Large porcupine quills also make very good flowing water sliders.

The shotting patterns for the still water and flowing water floats are very similar. The only difference being that for flowing water it is not necessary to have a single shot above the bulk shot (see Fig. 67C). The object of this shot when using an antenna float in still water is to keep the float clear of the bulk shot preventing tangles on the cast. Because the flowing water slider is attached to the line by two rings instead of just one, this problem does not occur.

It is very important to use a side or underhand cast when using sliding floats if tangles on the cast are to be avoided. It is also very important to cast into the wind, so when you practice your side casting, practice casting both from the right to the left and from the left to the right. You will then become competent at casting properly, no matter which way the wind is blowing.

The sliding pike float is the one exception to this. As split shots or shotting patterns are not needed, an overhead cast can be used, especially when you need to cast long distances. A piece of biro tube fitted through the centre of the float is ideal for this job. It is used in conjunction with the sliding stop knot and bead (see Fig. 69).

Due to the heavy nature of the tackle, a balsa bead will soon disintegrate, so a small plastic bead will work much better under these circumstances.

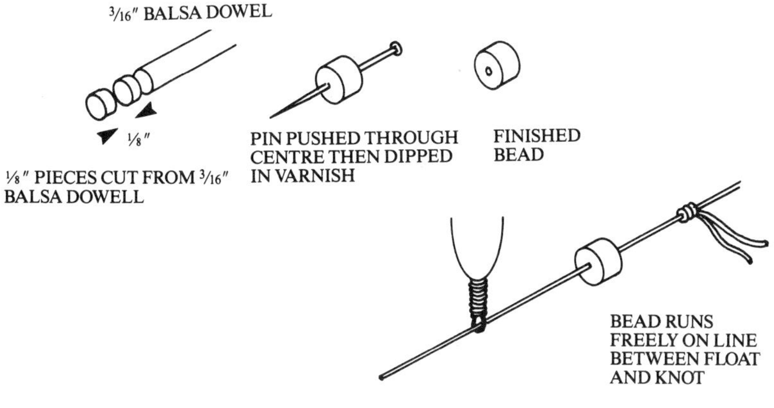

Fig. 68. Making a stop bead for sliders.

Fig. 69. Sliding pike rig.

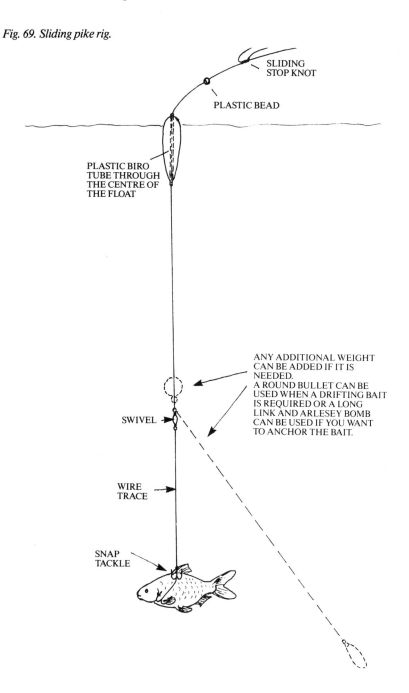

SLIDING
STOP KNOT

PLASTIC BEAD

PLASTIC BIRO
TUBE THROUGH
THE CENTRE OF
THE FLOAT

ANY ADDITIONAL WEIGHT
CAN BE ADDED IF IT IS
NEEDED.
A ROUND BULLET CAN BE
USED WHEN A DRIFTING BAIT
IS REQUIRED OR A LONG
LINK AND ARLESEY BOMB
CAN BE USED IF YOU WANT
TO ANCHOR THE BAIT.

SWIVEL

WIRE
TRACE

SNAP
TACKLE

The Sliding Stop Knot

It is important to learn this very simple but very versatile knot. Apart from its use as a stop knot when using sliding floats, it can also be used to make an adjustable link when link legering. This allows the leger angler to adjust his length of tail very quickly by moving the link up or down the main line.

The knot is formed by taking a separate piece of line approximately 6″ in length and normally of a higher breaking strain than the line you are using. This is then doubled over and laid along the reel line (see Fig. 70). One loose end is then taken and wrapped around the main line four or five times. The end is pushed through the loop you made when you first doubled the line over and the two ends are then pulled tight. The tighter you pull the more it will grip the line.

You are now left with your stop knot and the ends are about 3″ long. The natural thing to do would be to trim these ends neatly off, but it is important that this is NOT done. The ends should be left long to stop them catching in your rings when you cast. This would have a serious effect on your casting distance.

If an adjustable leger link is required, a longer length of line is needed to make the knot. After the knot has been tied, one end can be trimmed off leaving the one long length onto which you would tie your bomb (see Fig. 71).

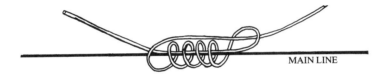

Fig. 70. The sliding knot.

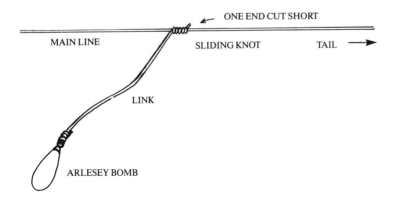

Fig. 71. Adjustable leger link.

111

Laying On and Float Legering

On many occasions when fishing flowing waters, especially in conditions of low water temperature and/or times of flood, the fish may be reluctant to take a bait trotted through in the normal way and will only take a static bait. In these conditions, laying on or float legering can be a very effective way of getting bites.

In slow or steady flowing water, this can be easily achieved by moving the float up a foot or two overdepth and the bottom shots up by the same amount, leaving a couple of feet of line laying on the river bed. Notice that I said you move the bottom shots up the line as well as the float. It is important to have the indicating shot clear of the bottom if this set up is to work efficiently (see Fig. 72).

This point is often overlooked by anglers who, after a period of trotting without results, resort to laying on tactics but only move the float up the line and ignore the terminal tackle.

In many cases the addition of extra shot immediately below the float or down the line with the bulk shot is also required. This is to prevent the float from riding too high in the water and to increase the sensitivity of the tackle.

Normally when laying on, the tackle is cast downstream and then held back in the current, allowing the tackle to straighten out and swing in towards the bank.

The rod is normally held straight out from the bank and supported by a rod rest. The distance from the bank at which the tackle lies is normally governed by the length of rod protruding out over the water (see Fig. 73).

Bites can often be induced by occasionally lifting the rod and allowing the tackle to inch itself downstream, covering a greater amount of the swim than if the tackle was just left in one position all the time. In this way it is possible to find 'HOT SPOTS' in the swim where the fish are lying. This may be due to an obstruction such as weed or rocks, or perhaps a shallow depression in the river

Fig. 72. Laying on.

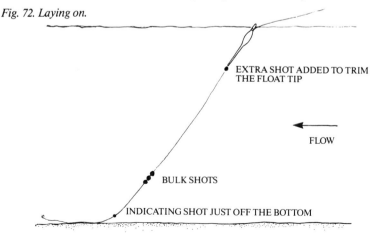

EXTRA SHOT ADDED TO TRIM
THE FLOAT TIP

FLOW

BULK SHOTS

INDICATING SHOT JUST OFF THE BOTTOM

bed. All of which provide shelter for the fish from the main flow. These cannot be seen by the angler from the bank, but by searching the length of the swim in this way they can be found by the sudden appearance of bites that only occur in these particular areas.

The advantage of laying on to legering is that the position of the bait can be easily pinpointed by the position of the float. The bait can be accurately placed over the hotspots much more easily than when legering.

When fishing fast or strong flowing water, laying on with float and shots becomes impractical because of the large amounts of fixed lead that need to be attached to the line to get the bait down to the fish and to set the float. The fish need to move all of this to indicate a bite and can feel the resistance caused by all this weight against the current. In these conditions legering methods need to be employed. But we can still keep the advantage gained by using a float to indicate the baits position in the swim as well as indicating the bite. This method is called float legering.

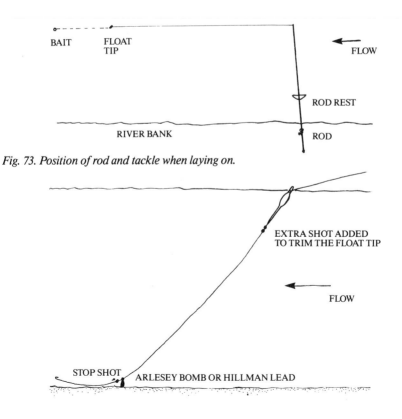

Fig. 73. Position of rod and tackle when laying on.

Fig. 74. Float legering in flowing water.

113

Fig. 75. Adjusting the line angle with the rod tip.

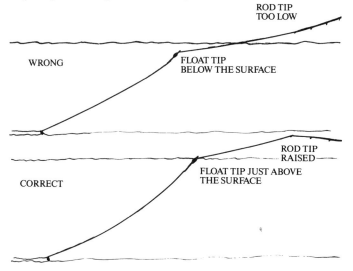

A Hillman lead or a small Arlesey bomb can be fixed onto the line and allowed to slide up and down the line freely. A leger stop or split shot can be fixed above the hook length giving the required length of 'tail' (see Fig. 74). Some split shot may still be needed to set the float tip to the required sensitivity but the bulk of the weight will be in the leger and it is important to set the depth accurately when using this method, taking into account the angle of the line. The weight will be on the bottom and the tip of the float just above the surface. By adjusting the angle of the rod tip to the float tip, small discrepancies in this distance can be counteracted (see Fig. 75). Only trial and error will teach you this. When using this method larger baits may sometimes be very effective. Match anglers will argue that when conditions are adverse, the tackle and bait size should be scaled down rather than up. But for general fishing I have often found the opposite to be the case. A large bunch of maggots, a worm, or a piece of bread flake will often produce a more positive bite on this kind of rig than a small bait fished on a small hook.

The best type of float to use when laying on or float legering in flowing water is the Avon type. The top buoyancy built into this design of float is essential if stability is to be achieved. The size of the float used is of course dependent upon the depth and strength of flow.

Float legering on still water is not so commonly used these days due to the great advances over the last few years in bite indicators. Even so, I think the method is worth covering as some anglers do get more pleasure from watching a float than a swing or quivertip. Also on some waters, it may be more practical to use float legering methods to overcome certain localised problems.

When float legering in still waters, the type of terminal tackle used is the same as when legering with a swing or quiver tip. A float of the antenna type is connected to the line above the tackle and is allowed to run freely up and down the line. It is stopped at the required setting by using the sliding stop knot described in the section covering sliding floats.

The distance between the terminal tackle and the float will be greater than the depth of the water (see Fig. 76A), and has to be set by trial and error. A rough guide to help with this setting would be to start at 1½ times the depth of the water although the distance from the bank at which we are fishing will be a contributory factor in deciding the position of the knot.

The rod is placed on the rod rest after casting and the final setting is done with the reel by adjusting the tightness of the line.

In waters that have a deep layer of either weed or mud on the bottom, this is a very good way of legering. Instead of having the hook length or tail longer than the bomb link which is normal when legering, the link is made much longer and the hook length is fixed paternoster style, this allows the bait to hang above the bottom (see Fig. 76B). This method is particularly effective when fishing for predators such as perch, pike or zander, with worm or small dead baits. It can of course, be used for other fish such as roach and bream using flake or maggot baits.

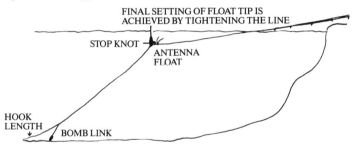

Fig. 76A. Float legering in still water.

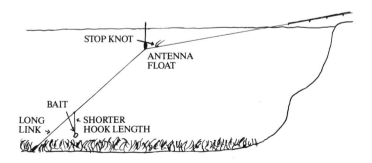

Fig. 76B. Paternoster rig for fishing a bait above weed.

The Lift Method

This method was devised to overcome the frustrations caused by bottom feeding fish such as tench, taking a bait into its mouth without moving the float sufficiently to justify the angler striking. A short piece of peacock quill is fastened to the line by the bottom end only. A single shot is positioned only two inches above the hook. The float is set overdepth, then cast in. The rod is placed on the rod rest and the line tightened to cock the float (see Fig. 77A).

When the bait is picked up by the fish, the shot is also lifted, causing the float to rise out of the water and then lie flat. Obviously for this to happen, the fish must be holding the bait and hook in its mouth, so you strike as soon as the float starts to lift (see Fig. 77B).

The size of the shot used is dependent upon the size of the quill and visa versa. A 4″ length of quill is a useful length to use, and the size of shot can be varied by using thicker or thinner pieces of quill as required. Do not be put off by the thought of having a AAA or SSG shot only two inches from the hook. The fish don't seem to worry, so why should you. When the fish are feeding confidently, the bite may be signalled in the normal way by the float going under, in which case you strike as usual.

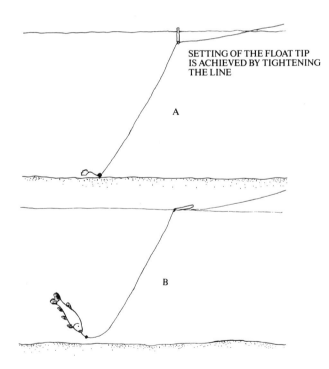

Fig. 77. The lift method.

This method is especially effective in shallow waters and where accurate casting close to weed beds, or into small holes in-between weeds is required. The single shot can be cast with much greater accuracy into these confined areas than if a complicated shotting pattern, or heavy float such as a dart or zoomer was used. The single shot precedes the float on the cast, whereas if a loaded float was used, the float would precede the terminal tackle, leaving the hooklength lying either over the weeds, or falling short of the required position.

Bolt and Hair Rigs

These rigs have been developed over the last few years, to overcome the problem of suspicious or shy biting fish producing unhittable bites or twitches, caused by the fish feeling the tackle and dropping or ejecting the bait within the split seconds between the angler seeing and reacting to the bite. Confidently feeding fish can also cause similar problems by taking the bait back into their throats and chewing it with their pharyngeal teeth and biting through the line. This is described by specimen anglers as a 'bite off'. They can be used either jointly or individually, depending upon the circumstances encountered.

The bait, instead of being attached to the hook, is moulded or threaded onto a fine piece of line, with a small piece of rubber tubing or cut up 'O' ring tied to one end to act as a stop. This is then tied to the bend of the hook using a blood knot (see Fig. 78). The length of the hair is determined by the size of fish you are expecting to catch. It can be from 20mm to 50mm in length. The fish then picks up the bait which is unencumbered by the weight or the presence of the hook on a stiff line, and as it takes it back into its throat to chew it, the bare hook is then drawn into its mouth. As the fish moves off, the stop hits the weight, causing the hook to prick and lodge in the inside of the mouth or lip (providing the hookpoint has been well sharpened), causing the fish to 'bolt', and giving the angler a positive and virtually unmissable indication. The strike will then drive the hook fully home. A larger than normally necessary leger weight is required to provide enough weight for the fish to pull against and many anglers shape the weight into a pyramid shape to give it more resistance to movement on a soft bottom. Old plummets make ideal bolt rig weights.

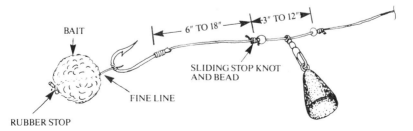

Fig. 78. Hair and bolt rig.

Touch Legering

Touch legering is a very effective method of fishing flowing water especially when using a rolling bullet to search a large area of the river bed. The bait and the leger are moving for most of the time, making a visual bite indicator such as a quiver tip very difficult to read. Also, when fishing for chub and barbel, particularly in the summer months, it is often essential if some degree of success is to be achieved, to fish into the late evening or at night. This also makes visual bite indication extremely difficult and if your sense of touch is developed by practising this method, then the rewards can be significant in terms of fish caught.

A light, properly balanced rod is essential if tiredness is to be avoided. After casting the rod should be held in the right hand at about 45° and the angler should be in a seated position. The butt can be held against your thigh or groin and after taking up any slack line, the line is pulled down from between the first two rod rings then held by the thumb and finger of the left hand. Some anglers prefer to use the forefinger whilst others use the second or third finger. The thing to do is experiment until you find which of your fingers is the most sensitive. If you are a left handed person then the reverse can be used.

Bites will be indicated by a series of plucks or trembles transmitted through the line, which of course, will be held under slight tension. The pressure of the moving water on the line and the terminal tackle will assist you to maintain this slight tension. You will soon distinguish after a bit of practice between the feel of the leger moving across the river bed and the pluck of a taking fish. Also, by regularly using this method, you will soon be able to determine the nature of the bottom, distinguishing between gravel and silt. It is very important especially when fishing for barbel, to know that your bait is lying on the type of bottom most attractive to the fish. Gravel being the favourite feeding area of the barbel. This method is only effective in flowing water. In still or very slow moving water, conventional visual indicators have to be used.

Dapping and Freelining

Often when fishing small streams and rivers which contain a wide variety of natural features, conventional float and leger fishing tactics can be either ineffective or impossible to use due to either the clarity of the water or the restrictions caused by the bankside vegetation. Under these conditions, freelining or dapping tactics can be very effective methods of taking good fish. One of the most appealing aspects of this style of fishing is that the hunting instinct inherent in all of us, is brought to the fore and satisfied to the full.

Fish location is the key to success on these types of water. The fish must be stalked and located and then all the ingenuity we possess must be employed to achieve their capture. Instead of the normal comfortable seated posture normally employed whilst fishing, the angler must achieve a wide number of unnatural positions to enable the bait to be presented to the fish without it being frightened or suspicious. This can include crawling along on your stomach or climbing up trees and poking your rod through the openings in the branches.

Planning your approach can also be a very fulfilling experience. First you must assess your approach to the fish and how you can get the bait to where the fish are lying in a natural and unsuspicious manner. You must then try to judge what the fishes reaction will be once it is hooked and make allowances for any alternative problems the hooked fish may present. It is no good getting the bait to the fish and hooking it if you are unable, due to the restricted area and bankside growth, to play and land it.

Large attractive baits such as slugs, lobworms, bread flake and crayfish, drifted down to a shoal of chub will often produce spectacular results. In clear water chub rely on their eyesight more when feeding than any of their other senses, and a large bait will often produce reaction from this species when small baits such as maggots and casters have been ignored.

Unlike the chub which will feed at all levels in the water, the barbel is mainly a bottom feeder. The bait may need to be left lying on the bottom close to a shoal of fish for some time before the fish will find it and take it.

Roach on the other hand, have an infuriating habit of ignoring any hook bait drifted down to them whilst making a meal of any free offerings loose fed into the swim. Bream, unless feeding, will totally ignore a bait altogether, especially in the summer months when they seem to spend most of the daytime sunbathing.

A lot can be learnt from observing the fish in these clear upper reaches of the rivers. This knowledge can be stored and used at various times in the year when due to the water being coloured because of spate or flood, fish location is more difficult.

When fishing in these snaggy and overgrown areas of the river, strong properly balanced tackle is essential. As I have explained in previous chapters, hook size and bait size, along with line strength and rod strength and action, go hand in hand if success is to be achieved. Line strength will not deter any fish as long as it is in proportion to the size of the hook and bait and the bait is presented properly. It is pointless reducing your line strength if the strength you are using is incapable of holding the fish away from any snags. Again what is the point of hooking a fish if you cannot land it.

The type of rod used when stalking fish in these snaggy areas is known as an Avon type rod. Because of the close range at which we fish in these conditions, it will have a through action to absorb the shock of the strike and the powerful lunges of the fish. A rod of 10 ft to 11 ft is normally used. A longer rod will only be an handicap in these restricted areas. The test curves will be higher than a normal float rod. They need to be 1 lb to 1½ lb to cope with lines from 4 to 8 lb B.S. which are the average line strengths for this type of fishing. A size 8 or 6 hook can be tied direct to the mainline and these should be of the forged type for extra strength. Lobworms, bread flake or slugs will easily cover this size of hook. If large baits such as crayfish or bunches of lobworms are used, then size 4 or 2 hooks may be needed.

The bait may need to be cast either upstream or downstream, depending on the accessibility allowed by the bankside growth. Bite indication can be either by seeing the bait being taken by the fish, or if fishing upstream and across, by the tightening of the 'bow' in the line. When fishing downstream, the bites can be detected by feel, or by the line tightening, or by rod tip indication. Only experience will teach you what to look for as no two bites will be the same.

Dapping is often a very effective method when fish are feeding off the surface. Baits can be natural large flies such as mayflies, sedgeflies and moths or pieces of breadcrust can be used. The bait is lowered on to the surface of the water using rushes or trees as cover. When using large natural flies, the dance of the sedgefly can be simulated by lifting the bait on and off the surface of the water. This can be very attractive to the fish and will often produce a very powerful and vicious take.

When using these tactics, polorised glasses are essential for fish and snag spotting beneath the surface glare. Always join the stems of the glasses with cord or elastic to prevent loss if they should slip off your ears whilst peering into the depths.

Never climb trees that overhang the water to spot fish unless you have a companion with you. If you slip or fall into the water in these remote parts of the waterside, it may well cost you more than just a soaking.

13 MATCH FISHING

Match fishing can be at many different levels, from a friendly bet amongst a small group of pleasure anglers, to a top class invitation match with hundreds of pounds at stake. But a successful match angler would approach both levels with the same degree of commitment.

Before any angler can consider successfully competing at any level, he must be capable of performing every function fluently and without conscious thought. He must be an angling machine, the epitome of efficiency and speed. Every action must be smooth and controlled. His equipment must be of the best quality and laid out in an orderly and efficient manner. This frees his mind to concentrate on the business of amassing the highest possible weight from the given stretch of water in front of him in the time available. He cannot choose his swim, or the time of day he can fish. During the summer months, the usual match time of 10am until 3pm is considered the worst time of day to catch fish. He starts when the fish have normally gone off the feed, and finishes before they are due back on again, the worst of both worlds.

Unless he has fished that swim before in similar conditions, which is a rare occurence for most matchmen, he must establish the geography of the swim, assess the potential in species and possible top weight, and then decide upon the best approach with regard to the conditions prevailing. It is here that the difference between the occasional match angler and the top class regular will become apparent.

The occasional matchmen will decide upon an approach, but if after a period fish are not forthcoming, doubt will creep into his mind and he will start to panic. Soon he will try every different weapon in his armoury, and every possible line in the river. Sometimes this may pay off, and the right method and lie of the fish located, but this may be because the initial choice of method or reading of the swim was wrong. Also the chances are that if this method then ceases to bear fruit, another method and line will be adopted.

Meanwhile, the regular matchman, confident he has chosen the right method, will be steadily building up his swim. He will feel confident that when the fish do move in and start to feed, he will have prepared his swim well and the fish will settle down and start to feed confidently. He will still feed the same line and possibly a second reserve line well away from the original, but he will constantly change his depth and shotting pattern to try and locate the depth at which the fish may be feeding. Slowly at first he will catch the odd fish; then gradually he will build up his catch rate. His bait and tackle will have been in the water for the maximum period during the match, and nothing that swims that has been slightly responsive to his bait will have been missed. During the last hour, the four hours of preparation will be paying off.

At the end of the match the other angler will be packing up, busily dismantling a number of rods and poles. He will have spent half the match out of the water whilst constantly changing methods and tackle. He will have caught a few fish, but at what expense with regard to time lost and effort wasted? Fish live in the water not on the bank, so unless the tackle is in the water you cannot catch them.

Eventually, this angler will gain in experience and have more confidence in his initial assessment of a swim and stick by it. He already has the versatility, he just needs to learn and control its application.

Once an angler has learnt to use and apply the vast range of methods available to him, he is ready to pit his ability against his fellow anglers. The secret is not to try to run before you can walk. Like any other form of angling, you must serve your apprenticeship first before you can reap the rewards. To start competing at open level before you have measured yourself against the best of the anglers at club level will prove costly in both financial terms and to your confidence and pride. The costs of fishing at open level are getting increasingly higher. Petrol and bait costs for both match and practice sessions must be met. The same amount of bait must be used on practice sessions as in the match if a realistic appraisal is to be made. On the day you will have entry fees and pools to find, and unless some regular return by means of prize money is forthcoming to subsidise these costs, the average angler would find regular open match fishing beyond his reach.

Most anglers start match fishing at club level. The travel costs are low as this normally involves fishing local club waters, or 30 or so anglers sharing the cost of a coach to the more distant venues. The pools are generally nominal and the whole event is normally well natured friendly rivalry for low stakes, the pride and prestige of winning being more important than the financial returns. Even so, the motivation and the will to win must be just as strong in the determined would-be match angler if he is to stand any chance on the open circuit.

Due to the rapid improvement of equipment, and the free flow of information on methods and tactics by the experts in the angling press, the standard of ability in the average club angler has increased immeasurably over the last five years. This in turn is reflected in the quality of anglers competing on the open circuit. Ten years ago, when travel and bait costs were lower in real terms, and venues more patchy in fish population, a good angler with a good draw was only competing against ten per cent of the field. In these days of pollution free rivers, with a more widespread and varied fish population, combined with a more knowledgeable and competent opposition, the average match angler finds the odds a lot less in his favour. Fluke results due to extreme conditions still give some hope to the average matchman, but more and more it is the same small group of top class anglers who consistently win, or get places in the big opens.

So it is even more important now to find the level at which you can remain a force to be reckoned with. If you have been consistent at being in the top three places at club level, try the local association matches at your local venues.

Once you have then secured a regular placing in section and match wins you can start to move further afield, selecting venues you are familiar with, and that need to be approached by your strongest methods. If you then wish to progress further, you must look at your range of approaches and methods and decide which points are your weakest. Is it pole fishing, or using a waggler at long range? Are you good at swingtipping but find swim feeders on flowing water a problem? Once you have identified your weaknesses, concentrate on them, and practice them until they become your strengths. Many anglers fail to study their "turn round time" for rebaiting or repairing tackle breakages. Most of the time spent out of the water for these and other things like hook changes, must be analysed and improved upon if you want to be successful. This may be the edge you may have on an angler fishing next to you whose catch rate is as fast as yours, but who may take a second or two longer to get his bait back into the water. These seconds become minutes in a five hour match, and minutes may mean an extra 1 lb of fish in the net at the end of the day.

No one can tell you how to become a top class match angler, most are born rather than made. I defy any man to define the quality that is in Ivan Marks over and above his outstanding knowledge, tackle handling and experience, but which is missing in his equally experienced, but less successful rival. All I can attempt to do with this chapter is to guide you along the path to the limits of your future ability.

The average length of a fishing match is five hours, but the dedicated matchmen will need to put in many times this short period in preparation for the event. Before going to a venue to practice, particularly if it is a water he does not fish regularly, he will need to collect as much information as possible about its current form, section variations, successful methods and baits. His sources of information will be the angling press, the match regulars 'grapevine', or by chatting with local anglers he finds on the bank when he goes on his practice session.

The practice session will consist of applying the information he has gathered, but using it only as a guide. He must, if he is to stand any chance on the day, adapt and improve on it, to give himself an edge on the opposition. He will be only too aware that his rivals will be doing their own homework. He will also realise that on the day, the fish will be far less responsive than in mid week with the banks relatively deserted. The same methods may not work, and a different bait may be needed. Also, the conditions on the day could be completely different. If it is a river, it may be carrying extra water, or have run off extra water and be clear instead of slightly coloured. The wind may be blowing a gale or be from a different direction, or if it is winter a severe overnight frost could cause a rapid fall in water temperatures. A practice session can only be useful when these considerations are taken into account.

Quite often the experienced angler can learn more by walking the banks and getting a feel for the water and chatting to the local anglers, than by isolating himself and his thoughts by just fishing a likely looking spot all day long. Practice sessions to the experienced matchmen means developing new methods and tactics and perfecting them for use when the conditions dictate. Using tried and tested methods, even on a new water, to the exclusion of any other considerations, cannot be deemed as practising in reality. This is one of the biggest pitfalls that the occasional match angler falls into. He is content to bask in the pleasant memories of when everything went right, instead of analysing and correcting the mistakes he made when things went badly wrong.

Much of the week prior to a match must also be dedicated to the preparation of the bait and tackle. Many of the top matchmen breed much of their own hookbait. I shall not go into the technicalities of this process, as much has already been written about this in most of the many excellent books on match fishing that have been written in recent years, and which any prospective match angler must consider as compulsory reading. The object of this chapter is to outline qualities and attitudes an angler must develop if he wishes to consider entering this complex and demanding aspect of the sport.

Commercial bait, if carefully selected and prepared, will be quite adequate for club level match fishing. The same degree of preparation is also essential for the pleasure angler, if consistent success is to be achieved. Commercial maggots must be sieved and put into fresh bran to remove any grease, and any dead maggots and skins separated. This will also remove most of the odour of the feed from the bait. This is especially essential if you wish to dye your own bait, as the colouring agents will refuse to take if the slightest hint of grease is still present. Several changes of bran or maize meal may be needed to achieve this. It can easily be obtained from pet stores or corn merchants.

If you require casters, and the regular quality from your local tackle shop is in doubt, then you must be prepared to 'turn' your own. This is fully described in the chapter on baits. Top matchmen always prepare their own casters to ensure both quality and quantity are available when they require them. Obviously, this means buying in a large amount of maggots, or having understanding neighbours who will tolerate a mini bait farm in their midst.

Tackle preparation is just as essential as the attention lavished on the bait. All equipment must be examined carefully for damage or wear, and a check kept to ensure that sufficient quantities of small consumable items such as hooks, shots, and leger weights are maintained. Line should be checked and replaced on a regular basis, and reels should be cleaned and checked and returned to the manufacturers for servicing each close season. Rod rings and reel line guides should be examined for wear and grooving, and nets checked for fraying due to abrasion, which can develop into holes and cost you a placing due to your hard earned fish escaping. A tidy and well laid out tackle box will reveal at a glance any reduction or losses in essential items. Regular checks and inspections will reveal any problems prior to rather than during a match.

As you can see, the dedication and determination required to succeed in match fishing is high, and unless you and your immediate family are prepared to uphold the commitment in both time consuming and financial terms, and be single minded in your will to succeed, then match fishing at an open level should not be considered lightly.

14 FISHING FOR BIG FISH

It is within the capability of any angler to catch big fish. The only reason many anglers do not catch them is because they do not set out to do so.

They generally fish with normal float tackle using small baits on small hooks. As there are far more small fish than there are big fish, obviously the small fish find the bait first. Occasionally a big fish will beat the small ones to the bait, but because the angler is using light tackle and is not prepared or experienced in handling large fish on fine tackle, the odds are normally 10-1 in the fishes favour. How then do you go about catching big fish?

The most important thing to do is to find a water which contains them. This may seem obvious, but it's surprising how many people fish a water regularly without really knowing its full potential.

The second thing to do is cut down the chances of small fish taking the bait first. To do this you must use baits that are too large or of a type that small fish will not take.

Once you have located your water and determined what species of quality fish it holds, you must then locate the feeding areas of the fish you want to catch. These areas can vary as to the time of the day and the season of the year. They can only be located by accurate information. This can be obtained from local anglers but it can, even at the best of times, be rather unreliable. The best information is obtained by your own observations.

In the summer months, especially on still waters, the fish tend to fall into a regular feeding pattern along various parts of the water. They will completely avoid certain areas for reasons best known to themselves, and stick to a particular route around the various areas that they do inhabit. They patrol these areas either individually or in a shoal. The individual fish tend to be the larger, older fish. They sometimes shadow a shoal of their smaller brethren, keeping back out of the way until they are ready to move into the area after the others move off. This is often why when fishing for large fish, several smaller fish will be caught before the larger fish start to show.

Once these feeding routes have been located, observation will give you some idea of the time of day the fish move through a particular area. You can then bait up the area well before the fish are due to arrive, then lie in wait ready to ambush the shoal at the appointed hour.

What then are the signs to look for when locating these areas? If the water is clear you can actually see the gaps in the weed which the fish move through. Also if you are still and quiet you can see the fish under the water by using polaroid glasses. Fish are attracted to weed beds, sandy bars, shelves and ledges, or by the type of bottom in which they know holds food. The large bottom feeders such as carp, tench and bream, often give their position away by the clouds of bubbles they send up whilst rooting around on the bottom for food — an important sign for fish location in cloudy waters. Also rushes or weeds are moved as fish pass through them or ripples are caused as they brush against the stems of lily pads.

The most popular feeding areas of tench and carp are in the margins of the lake or pond. In the evenings and early mornings they move into the margins and patrol along them in search of food, providing that is, that there is no bankside disturbance. During the day the fish tend to lie up in the middle of the water, especially in the hot weather and do not start feeding until the sun has gone off the water. Then they start to move into their feeding areas, patrolling the water in their set patterns. A typical feeding route is shown in Fig. 18. This shows a lake and its various features, with the probable feeding areas of the different species of fish that the lake may hold.

In the summer months, when water temperatures are high, the best time to catch big fish is normally in the early morning and late evening. On cloudy days the feeding time of the fish is often prolonged, but generally as soon as the sun hits the water with any sort of intensity the fish stop feeding. Once this happens your only chance of an odd fish during the daytime is to fish in a shady or deep part of the lake in the hope of picking up an odd fish as they move into these areas. The exception to this is when carp fishing.

Carp are more likely to move into any reed beds around the margins of the water provided there is no bankside disturbance, especially on hot sunny days. They lie in these areas basking in the sun on, or near the surface of the water. A piece of crust lowered or cast gently onto the surface of the water will often be taken by a carp, providing you are very quiet and blend into the background.

Obviously when fishing for carp in these very snaggy areas, very strong tackle is needed. Strong line and a large hook are useless unless a strong rod is used as well. The type of rod used in these circumstances is what is known as a stepped-up carp rod. This is to say that the test curve of the rod is much stronger than that of a normal carp rod.

It is very important to learn about rod actions and test curves, especially if you want to be successful in catching big fish. It is not fair to the fish, yourselves or to other anglers, if you go after big fish with inadequate or badly balanced tackle. It will only result in lost fish and hardship to those fish left to swim around with hooks and long lengths of line hanging from their mouths. So, let's have a look at the type of tackle required to catch large fish.

A normal float rod has a test curve of about 12 ozs. This means that the amount of weight needed to bend the rod tip to an angle of 90° is 12 ozs (see Fig. 79). This rod will cope with line of up to 4 lbs B.S. and hook sizes up to size 10. If heavier line or larger hooks are used with this rod, the rod will be over-loaded and any advantage thought to be gained from using this heavier tackle will be lost. If a line of heavier strength is needed a rod with a stronger test curve is required. A normal float rod with a line strength up to 4 lbs B.S. is quite adequate for fishing in snag free waters for roach, tench, bream, barbel and chub, up to a weight of 3 lb. For larger fish of these species, or for fishing in snaggy waters where a lot of pressure needs to be applied to the fish to prevent it from reaching these snags and breaking your line, a rod with a test curve of

1 lb to 1¼ lb is needed. This rod is designed to handle line strengths of 4 lbs to 8 lbs B.S. and hook sizes to size 6.

When fishing for carp, pike and zander, a rod capable of handling heavier line and casting heavy baits is needed. For line strengths of 8-12 lbs B.S. and for fishing at close to medium range, a rod with a test curve of 1½-2 lbs is ideal. For heavier lines of 12 lbs upwards, a series of stepped up rods with test curves of 2½ lbs upwards are required. For fishing at long range they need to be stiff in their action. This is so they can pick up a long length of line quickly and set the hooks firmly into a fish.

If you are fishing at close range, a rod with a soft action will be needed, otherwise the hooks will be ripped out of the fishes mouth when pressure is applied. A soft rod absorbs the lunges of the fish. At long range the line will cushion the strike and the playing of the fish, so a stiff rod is needed to keep in contact and to set the hooks. If a soft rod was used, the combination of the line stretch and the soft rod would make control of the fish and the setting of the hooks at long range an impossible task.

A soft action rod has a through action. A stiff fast taper rod has a tip action (see Fig. 80). This describes where the rod bends. With a soft through action, the rod will curve all the way along, right down to the handle in extreme cases. A tip action rod, due to its steep taper, bends only from the tip to the middle of the rod, the lower part of the rod will remain relatively straight.

Most of your fishing will be done at close to medium range, so the type of rods you will be needing to start your fishing will be the through action type. These can be bought in lengths of 10-11½ ft. Most anglers who specialise in catching large fish, make up their own rods from blanks. This is by far the cheapest way of obtaining a good rod. Most good dealers carry a range of rod blanks of various test curves and actions. You can also buy them part built. This means that the handles are fitted and shaped and all you have to do is whip on the rings and varnish it. You can save up to £10 or more per rod if you are prepared to do your own whipping. This is fully described in the section on tackle making.

You will very seldom use a float when fishing for big fish, except for tench, roach and pike. In most situations, legering or freelining is the most popular and effective way to catch big fish. For this reason a rod longer than 11 ft is unnecessary. If you refer to the following chart you will see the balance of rod strengths, line strengths and hook size to the various species of fish. Use this guide and you will not go far wrong. Remember that a fast taper stiff actioned rod is for long range fishing only. A through action rod is the ideal type for most other forms of fishing.

Species	Test Curve	Line Strength	Hook Size
Bream Roach Perch Crucian Carp	¾ lb	2-4 lb	22-10
Bream Tench Chub Barbel Perch	1-1¼ lb	5-8 lb	10-6
Carp Pike Zander	1½-2½ lb	8-15 lb	6-2
Carp Pike	2½ lb +	15 lb +	6-2

A good quality reel with ball or roller bearings is essential when fishing for big fish. A small cheap reel will just not stand the pressure sometimes required when playing big fish. The gears will just strip off and the reel will soon start to break up. A good reliable reel is a must.

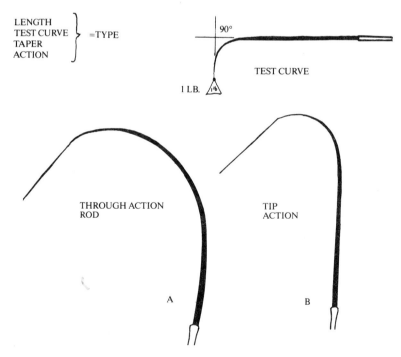

Fig. 80. Rod actions.

Line must be changed more frequently than when general fishing. This is because it will lose its stretch much quicker due to the amount of pressure sometimes put upon it when playing big fish. Also it must be checked for fraying or other damage before each outing.

Hooks are normally tied direct to the main line; they must be checked for sharpness and temper before use and sharpened with a stone if they feel blunt. Never use a hook that has any rust or corrosion on the point or shank. Always keep them in packets. Do not allow them to rattle around loose in a tin.

So you have located your fish, you have got the correct tackle, how do you go about catching them?

This depends to a great deal upon the range you need to fish and the type of bait you are using. If you intend to use a large paste bait at fairly close range, then there is little point in using a link leger. The weight of the bait is sufficient to reach the area you want to fish, so the addition of more weight will serve no useful purpose and could be a handicap. At best it will do nothing, at worst it may cause tangles and make a splash when entering the water, scaring the fish away. So the main thing to remember is, keep it simple.

If you are fishing bread flake or worm or some other light bait, a link leger must be used. This can be made up of a couple of swan shots on a link or the correct type of leger weight as required. The leger is tied onto a short length of nylon, about 3″-6″ long, with a ring or a swivel tied to the end. The main line is then fed through the ring so that the link can slide freely up and down the line (see Fig. 42). You must then slide a stop onto the line. This can be one of the type now on sale in most tackle shops, or you can make your own using a piece of plastic or rubber tube locked onto the line with a piece of tapered matchstick. A short piece of Biro tube is ideal for this purpose. The best method to avoid any chance of weakening the line is to use a sliding knot and bead (see Fig. 78).

At no time should you use split shot. This will damage and weaken your line, probably causing you to lose a good fish. The leger should be stopped about 2-3 ft from the hook which is whipped onto the line after you have fitted up your link and stop.

Bite indication can be achieved in several ways. A simple method is to use a dough bobbin or silver paper fitted onto the line between the butt ring and the second ring (see Fig. 109). This is a very effective method when confident runs are expected. When fishing with more than one rod, or when night fishing, an electronic bite alarm is a very useful piece of equipment. This is used in conjunction with the butt indicator. (See Fig. 81). When a fish picks up the bait or noses the bait the line will tighten. This causes the feeler on the electronic indicator to move across and make contact. This contact then activates the alarm. The butt indicator will then tell you at what rate the bite is developing. Sometimes the alarm noise and the rising of the indicator will be instantaneous. At other times the alarm will sound at the initial tightening of the line but it will be several minutes before the run develops and the indicator rises.

Indicators can be made of all sorts of materials, the easiest to make is by using the top off a washing up liquid bottle. This can be used just as it is, or mud or groundbait can be pushed into the bottom to weight it (see Fig. 109). A Beta light can also be fixed into the bottom for night fishing. Beta lights are small glass vials filled with tritium gas and can be fitted onto swing tips, floats or into bobbins. They send out a very powerful light and do not need recharging with light like the old type luminous floats. They are very expensive but are a worthwhile investment if you intend doing a lot of night fishing.

The type of bobbin I favour is made from a hairgrip. Onto the hairgrip you can glue either a Beta-light or a piece of silver paper. You then tie a piece of thick nylon or string onto the back end and connect this to a meat skewer or tent peg (see Fig. 110). The grip is then clipped onto the line. When a run occurs the grip will be pulled off the line when the rod is picked up. I adopted this method after experiencing a washing up liquid bottle top wrapping itself around the rod on the strike, causing the line to jam. This resulted in the loss of the biggest fish of the night.

If the fish are biting shy, or if you are fishing for roach, the swingtip is a good indicator on still waters. But you can only fish with a single rod when using a tip. You cannot use a bite alarm with a swing tip or rod end indicator and it is impossible to concentrate on two tips at the same time and still fish effectively. This will only result in missed bites or badly hooked fish, a thing to avoid whenever possible. If you use a swingtip with a Beta-light attached for night fishing, you must use a second light as a *target* light. This would be fixed onto a bank stick and be positioned along side the light on your swing tip, giving a fixed point to indicate any movement of the light on your tip. Otherwise you could miss a lot of very gentle bites which would not be seen without a target light. Your eyes play some very funny tricks when staring at a tiny point of light in pitch darkness.

If you are using flake or paste baits, and they are beginning to lose their effectiveness, you may want to try particle baits such as sweetcorn. The thing to do is feed several areas along the fishes feeding path over a period of a week or so, then when conditions seem right, fish with the bait in those areas. Never expect a change of bait to work wonders. It may take extensive pre-baiting before results occur, but once the fish do accept it, good sport can be enjoyed. When fishing large baits in flowing water such as bread crust or flake, use large shots near the hook if necessary to sink the bait. A typical float fishing rig for use with large baits in fast flowing water is shown in (Fig. 37).

When fishing for tench or carp, water temperatures play a very important part. One of the reasons early morning is a noted time for the fish to start feeding is because it is at that time of day water temperatures are near their highest. After a hot sunny day the heat absorbed by the ground is then absorbed by the water through the bed of the pond or lake. Air temperatures and surface ground temperatures will drop during the night, but the water temperature will still be high. This is why you see mist rising off the lake in the early morning. This generally is always a good sign. Very still cloudy nights also seem to be better for bites than cold clear ones. Try to keep a log of water temperatures and weather conditions. Some sort of pattern for your waters may emerge giving you an edge over the other anglers. You may notice that in certain conditions the fish alter their feeding pattern or route. The reason why the normal hot spots may not have been fishing so well on certain days. Armed with this information, you can go to a swim where the fish may be in the prevailing conditions where normally they wouldn't show. Time spent observing the habits of your local fish can save you a lot of fishing time later on, so don't be over keen to get fishing and neglect your preparation and observation, it could cost you a lot of fish.

A large landing net and keep net, plus a set of good quality scales are important items if you intend to fish for big fish. Otherwise you may lose or damage your fish, and be unable to keep accurate records of your catches. Never hook fish under the gills with the scales, this causes serious injury to the fish. Always use a fine net or a plastic carrier bag to place your fish in whilst weighing. Always handle the fish carefully and never put them back without ensuring they have fully recovered. Support them in the water with their heads pointing upstream if in flowing water until they can swim away properly. barbel especially need this kind of assistance.

Pike and Zander

When fishing for pike and zander, the same basic methods of legering or freelining still apply. The main difference lies in the terminal tackle. Treble hooks and wire traces are essential items of terminal tackle. These are used only for pike and zander fishing in this country. This type of tackle is not needed for any other species of freshwater fish in the British Isles with the exception of large eels. The reason you need to use wire traces is because of the very sharp teeth that these fish have. They would very quickly cut through ordinary line. The treble hooks are used for two reasons, one is because the hooks are used to hold the bait securely as well as to hook the fish; secondly, these fish have very hard boney mouths and getting a hook hold is very difficult, so trebles are used to increase the chance of keeping the fish hooked.

The size of hooks is dependent to a large degree upon the size of the bait. If a gudgeon or small dace is used a size 12 or 10 is sufficient. If a herring or mackeral or a dead roach are used, a size 8 or 6 will be needed. Dead baiting is just as effective as live-baiting. In some cases where herrings and spratts are used it is more effective. The strong scent from these baits is very attractive to these fish. Live or dead baits are mounted on what is called a snap tackle, which in turn is connected to a wire trace. One of the most common of these is the Jardine snap tackle, which was named after the inventor and very famous pike angler Alfred Jardine. It consists of a length of stranded wire onto which are mounted two treble hooks. One is fixed, the other can slide up or down the wire to suit any size of dead bait. The lower fixed hook is inserted under the baits pectoral fin, the second sliding hook is fixed under the dorsal fin of the bait (see Fig. 69). They can be fished freelined or paternoster style, using a link leger. If fished in mid-water they can be suspended under a float.

That's something I had to cover because it's the Jardine snap which the angler will encounter as he goes into the average tackle shop. In fact experienced pike anglers nowadays make up their own traces with treble hooks and some of the excellent fine twisted wire which is now available from specialist suppliers, some of whom also market much more up-to-date traces than the traditional 'snap'. I'll return to the specialist side of pike angling a little later.

Very little change has been made in the design of pike floats for many years, but the last few years have seen some progress. When I was a lad, the only type of floats we could buy for pike fishing were the type known as the Fishing Gazette bung. This was a very large, egg shaped float with a slot in the side into which the line was placed. The float was then secured onto the line with a peg which was pushed into the float, trapping the line. The peg would then swell up in the water making it very difficult to remove at the end of the day. For almost half a century this useless piece of equipment reigned supreme. They can still be bought today. Avoid Fishing Gazette bungs.

Some very good slim balsa or plastic pike floats are now on the market. For fishing at a distance I prefer the vaned type. This float is made so that a large area of colour is visible to the angler from any position but the actual cross sectional area is very small, offering no resistance at all to a taking fish (see Fig. 82). For fishing in deep water a sliding float is used. By deep water I really mean anything deeper than 5 ft, as to try and cast a heavy bait with a float set any deeper is almost impossible. These floats have a plastic tube down the centre and are stopped with a sliding bead and stop knot. This is the stepped

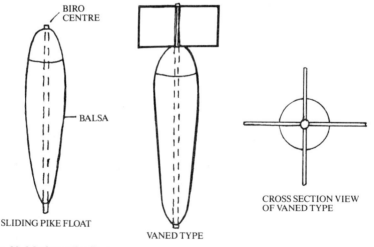

Fig. 82. Modern pike floats.

up version of the stop knot described in the chapter on advanced techniques. The main advantage in fishing a bait with a float as opposed to leger or freelining is that you can cover far more water due to the float fished bait drifting. This is a big advantage on large featureless lakes or pits where fish location is very difficult. But on lakes where obvious features help in the location of fish such as feeder streams, gulleys, weedbeds etc. then a legered or freelined bait is preferable. Two rods can be set up with bobbin indicators and with electronic alarms if possessed, and two probable areas can be fished at the same time. If using two rods, two different types of bait can be used to find out which will be the best bait for this particular session. If several bites come to one particular bait whilst the fish show no interest in the bait being fished on the second rod, then both rods can be set up with the successful bait and your chances of a run are doubled. When using more than one rod, the bail arms must always be left open on the reels, otherwise if your attention is elsewhere the rod can be pulled in by a taking fish. Also, a separate rod licence is needed for each rod.

Several items of specialist equipment are made for pike, and I find myself in immediate difficulty here. Anglers are still sold spring wire gags for holding the pike's lethal, toothy mouth open while the hooks are being removed. Experienced pike men abandoned this long ago, in favour of hand operation. This is difficult to describe, but it's possible to slide the hand into the gill cover of a pike and hold its mouth open without encountering its formidable teeth. A heavy duty gardening glove should be used by anyone who hasn't mastered the method, which is very much more kind to the pike than the barbarous gag. I would say the very best advice I could give beginners in pike fishing is to contact and join their nearest branch of the Pike Anglers Club. They would be shown how to handle pike properly, and how to fish for them efficiently and safely (i.e. the best rigs to use and how to time the strike to avoid harming the fish). It is one of the most specialised branches of the sport, and it's well worth joining the PAC and starting on the right foot. Even when holding a pike's mouth open properly you still need long artery forceps for removing deep-set hooks, and at the same time keeping the unhooking hand clear of the teeth.

Always use a large landing net for pike and zander. Do not use a gaff. Gaffs are used when the fish being caught are always killed for the pot, such as salmon and sea fish. Do not kill pike and zander, they are not vermin. They form a natural part of the balance of nature. They have as much right to life as a carp or roach and should be given the same respect by anglers. Do not let yourself be talked into killing pike by other less enlightened anglers. If you catch it then you are responsible for its well-being. Return it to the water as soon as possible, causing it the minimum of distress. Do not leave too long a period between when a run develops to when you strike. Pike do not always stop to turn the bait as many people believe they do. So do not wait for it to stop and then run a second time. This will only result in badly hooked fish. I normally count slowly to 10 then strike hard. I very seldom lose a fish. Hook penetration can be greatly improved by filing down the barbs on your hooks. Since I started to do this, my losses of fish have almost disappeared. Also it is far easier to unhook the fish afterwards.

Spinning is a very pleasant way of catching fish, especially pike. This is best done on a fairly deep snag free water. Spinners are very expensive items of tackle and are easily lost in shallow weedy water. To me, the loss of a good spoon always blights what otherwise was a good day. In some cases it is unavoidable, but if a bit of care is used these losses can be kept to a minimum. If you want to fish in shallow water, use a floating plug type lure. These are made of wood or plastic and are designed to float when the line is slack and dive when the line is retrieved. By varying the rate of retrieve, the action of the plug can be varied. Never just cast and wind in a plug or spoon. Try to make it more attractive by varying the rate of retrieve and by raising and lowering the rod top. The object of using a lure is to try and simulate the movements of an injured or dying fish. Dying fish do not speed through the water at 20 knots in a dead straight line. They wobble and pause at various intervals. As with snap tackle a wire trace is used between the lure and the main line.

Perch can also be taken using a small spoon or plug bait. But if you intend spinning for perch, scale and tackle down; 3 lb to 4 lb line, balanced to a lighter rod is ideal for perch. If you use the same heavy tackle for perch that you use for pike, you will lose a lot of enjoyment in playing the fish, plus the fact that the heavy line will restrict the action of a small lure and fewer bites will be forthcoming.

Fig. 81. Bite alarm with silver foil indicator on knitting needle.

15 NIGHT FISHING

There are many occasions when it pays an experienced angler to fish either into or through the hours of darkness if he wants to catch specimen fish. Many big fish do not move into their main feeding areas until the light level falls, because many of these areas are in the shallow water around the margins and sand and gravel bars on still waters, or along the shelves and ledges or in the shallow streamy areas on flowing waters.

During the day, particularly on heavily fished waters, the bigger fish tend to keep to the deeper, quieter parts of the lake or river, wary of natural predators and any bankside disturbance. In rivers, species such as large roach and barbel are very difficult to spot, even in very clear water. In still water, tench are seldom spotted moving around during the daytime, and the only clue to their whereabouts is given in the late evenings and early mornings by the clouds of tiny bubbles sent up by the feeding fish. This does not mean that specimen fish can only be caught at night. On the quieter stretches of water, a properly planned approach of location, correct feeding and presentation of the bait will often work well during the daytime, but due to the ever increasing amount of angling pressure being applied to many waters, then night fishing is often necessary if consistent results are to be obtained.

Some anglers fish through the night purely to ensure they secure and prepare the swim for the following mornings sport, particularly during the opening days of the season. In my area, the best tench swims on many still waters are taken up before lunch time on the day preceeding the opening day! Many cast in on the stroke of midnight, knowing they will remain fishless until the following dawn when the tench move in and start to feed. Tench like many other species seem to feed more heavily in the late evenings and early mornings, and although they can be caught during the hours of darkness, the biggest catches are normally taken after dawn and occasionally into the mid-morning on warm cloudy days. Late evening and a couple of hours after dusk is generally the best time to catch big roach and barbel during the summer and autumn months, but for big bream and carp, especially on heavily fished waters, then night time offers the best chances.

Many inexperienced anglers attempt to fish at night, totally unprepared in terms of tackle handling experience or planned approach, and either pack up by midnight, or struggle on into the cold light of the following dawn, vowing never to subject themselves to such an ordeal again.

Unless you are literally capable of carrying out every required function associated with angling with your eyes closed, then do not be a burden to yourselves or to your fellow anglers by attempting to fish at night.

When planning a night fishing session, the following guidelines should be considered: A thorough knowledge of the water and the swim to be fished is essential. Also you should know what species and size of fish are likely to be encountered, and have the proper tackle and experience to be able to cope. The method to be used must be familiar and completely mastered and the tackle and equipment well prepared. You must keep the set up as simple and as uncomplicated as possible.

Always get to your swim before it gets dark and set up your tackle so that everything is at hand without having to move from your seat. Always use a folding chair or bedchair in preference to a tackle carrier or basket. At night, comfort must be your priority. Always wear your warmest clothing and carry some spare extra clothing to put on if the temperature should fall lower than expected. Do not be too ambitious with the range at which you intend to fish. Try to find a swim where you can expect the fish to feed close in. Find out the geography of the swim before the light fades, noting the whereabouts of any shelves or other features, and marking them in your memory by using any reflections in the water of trees etc., as a guide. These will still be visible at night. Note the position of any weedbeds or other snags. Until you are experienced at night fishing avoid any really awkward swims and practice on the snag-free areas of the water.

When fishing at night, your senses become much more acute than when fishing in the daytime. It is surprising how much you will be able to see, even on the darkest of nights. Always take a torch with you to assist in the unhooking of the fish, but never shine it over the water, or into the eyes of other anglers who are fishing. Make sure that essential items such as forceps and hook disgorgers are placed in a prominent position.

I have found by experience that the most productive times are from before dusk to around 1 am. After this time until around dawn, things usually go dead. I use the word 'usually' guardedly. In angling, nothing is ever consistent or predictable and exceptions to any rule are always on the cards. But if, for example, you have to work the following day, and you need to snatch a few hours sleep, then this is the best time to indulge. Always remove your tackle from the water and your bait from the hook before nodding off, unless you are using an electronic bite alarm with a well amplified signal and know from experience that you will react to it quickly. Otherwise the result could be a badly deep-hooked fish, or if the tackle is removed from the water and the bait left on, a distressed and ferocious mammal such as a rat or vole, connected to your rod and line.

Never move around the bankside unnecessarily. A stumble or fall could leave you unconscious, face down in the waters margin at worst, or with a broken or sprained limb, it could result in exposure during cold conditions, and your being helpless on a deserted bank miles from any assistance. At best you could end up soaked to the skin and have to abandon the session. Always make sure someone knows where you will be fishing, and when you are likely to return.

The methods and tackle described in the chapter on Fishing for Big Fish are, due to their simplicity, the best to use when you first start night fishing. A silver paper indicator is still visible even on the darkest night, but if you intend to take it seriously and invest in bite alarms etc., then a more sophisticated set up with a Beta-light in the indicator will be preferable to silver paper on a knitting needle.

There are two basic types of electronic bite alarms. The simplest and cheapest type is where the line is passed around a tensioned wire feeler which is connected to a contact point. When the line is tightened by a fish taking the bait, the feeler is moved across and the contact completes the electrical circuit, activating the alarm. The more efficient but expensive type has a roller device. As the line is pulled forwards, the roller rotates and a tiny blade passes across the field of a photo-electric cell, interrupting the circuit and causing the alarm to bleep. Unlike the feeler type, this is a true bite alarm and indicator, as the rate at which the alarm bleeps is an indication of the rate at which the line is moving. This is approximately one bleep for each 20mm of line movement. With the feeler type of alarm, the contact is made by the line tightening. An additional Indicator is needed to show the actual rate of line movement. (See Fig. 81). Much more detailed information on methods and equipment can be found in the many excellent books on modern specimen fishing that are now available.

16 TACKLE MAKING

Many anglers go through their whole lives convinced they are incapable of replacing a broken rod ring or even whipping their own hooks, preferring to buy everything ready made, or to pay their tackle dealer for any repairs they may need doing. This is all very well if you are content to lay out vast amounts of extra money over the years and rely on other peoples handiwork. The most important thing these anglers are losing cannot be calculated in terms of hard cash or lost time and fish due to bad workmanship. This is the vast amount of satisfaction and pleasure gained from catching fish on tackle of your own design, made by yourself with all the care and attention you have personally put into it.

I can still remember to this day the pleasure I derived from seeing my very first home made float go under for the first time, with the satisfying thump of a nice plump roach crowning my first tackle making achievement. I can also remember the sadness I experienced when one day several seasons later, I saw that same float disappearing under the water for the last time, trailing several feet of loose line behind it. The loss of an old and dear friend. These emotions would never have been experienced if it had been just another shop bought float.

By my present standards that first float was a very rough and ready affair. The paint work and finish was very rough and the body was far from symmetrical, but it was my first step along the road to a happy angling career and it caught me a lot of fish.

For the beginner, as well as being an important part of your angling apprenticeship in terms of pleasure and achievement, it will play an important role in building up your tackle collection at a minimum of cost. Once you have bought the basic items such as rods, reels, nets, shots and hooks, then providing you have a go at making and repairing your own gear, your only costs will be permits, day tickets, bait and replacement of line and hooks. Most materials for tackle making, especially for floats, can be found, scrounged, or bought for just a few pence.

Float Making

I will deal with float making first as it is the simplest and cheapest way to start tackle making. The end product is achieved quickly and can be tried out immediately. Success in this department will soon build up your confidence to try more complicated tasks and the cost of failure is virtually nil. Do not be put off by early failures. We all have them and they are essential if experience is to be gained. Follow the basic patterns I am going to suggest and your failures should be minimal.

First of all, we will need a few basic tools and equipment, most of which are normal household items.

You will need the following: A pair of pliers, a sharp modelling knife or razor blade, medium and smooth sandpaper, some fine wet and dry paper (used for preparing car paint work), some nails of various diameters (2 mm, 3 mm and 4 mm), a pair of scissors, some small drills (2 mm, 3 mm and 4 mm if possible), some 15 amp fuse wire, a block of expanding polystyrene (as used for packing Hi-Fi equipment, radios, T.V.'s etc.). A couple of paint brushes, (medium and fine), a bottle of turps, a tin of matt black, matt white and fluorescent red paint, a spool of whipping silk and a tin of varnish (non cellulose). Two types of adhesive are also needed. Balsa cement and rapid setting Araldite.

Most of these items are obvious as regards to their function. Others like the polystyrene need explaining. This item is used for sticking the floats into whilst the adhesive or paint is drying. A cardboard box with holes punched in it can be used instead but it is not as efficient.

The reason I have suggested matt paint is that it dries quicker than gloss paint and as the float is to be sealed with varnish, the use of gloss paint is not necessary. Cellulose paints, although they are fast drying should be avoided. They dry brittle and easily crack up and flake off when the floats are in use. Also if cellulose paint or varnish is used on top of enamel paint it will cause it to bubble up. Normally only two colours are needed for float tips, matt black or matt fluorescent red. Avoid gloss fluorescent paint. It is difficult to apply and it does not show up as well as the matt. The 15 amp fuse wire is used to make the float rings.

Now for the float making materials themselves. Bird quills, though not used very much by the float manufacturers these days, are the cheapest and easiest materials to use. The reason the manufacturers do not use them is that due to their variation in shape and diameter, they are uneconomical to mass produce. Only peacock quill, due to its fairly even diameter and relative straightness is used. Although quills have fallen out of favour with the float manufacturers for purely economic reasons, they figure very highly in the estimation of anglers who prefer to make their own floats.

Crowquills can be found lying in the fields in almost every part of the country and swan and heron quills are often found at the waterside. Whole or parts of these quills are all very useful for float making and they should always be picked up and collected when you see them. Peacock quill can be bought at most good tackle shops and one length of quill can be used to make 4 or 5 floats with bits left over that can be kept for use as inserts in other types of material.

Sarkandas reed — this material was introduced in the early 1970's as a peacock substitute during a peacock quill famine. It is less buoyant than peacock and it is very difficult to get a coat of paint to stay on without it cracking off. Apart from this, it is a very good material to work with and makes excellent inserts for waggler and antenna floats. If you lightly sand it, and a coat of varnish is applied before painting and then a second coat put on over the paint, this will normally hold. It's only when you try to paint directly onto the reed that problems with adhesion occur.

Balsa wood is the next most popular material and can be used on its own or in conjunction with quills, cane or wire, to produce a wide variety of floats. 10 mm, 12 mm and 15 mm balsa dowel can be drilled and shaped for use as bodies on Avons, wagglers, or antenna floats. Ready drilled and shaped balsa bodies can also be bought from tackle shops, but these are more expensive than if you can shape your own. 4 mm, 6 mm and 8 mm balsa dowel is used for making the bodies of stick floats and trotting floats. Cork bodies can also be bought ready drilled and shaped from shops, but with practice you can make your own from wine corks. This material is better than balsa for use with quill floats. But when cane stems are to be used, balsa bodies are superior in performance.

Piano wire is now widely used for the stems of stick floats. It comes in various gauges, but for float making gauges 22, 20 and 18 are used. This can be bought from any model making shop quite cheaply.

Brazing rod. This brass material is the best for use as stems in floats where 'loading' is required for casting long distances. 16 s.w.g. and 10 s.w.g. are the useful sizes. It can be obtained from tool shops. Nails or splitpins can be used as an alternative, but only in the last resort as these can rust after a period of time.

Cane. A widely used material for stems of Avon or antenna floats. 2 mm dia. and 3 mm dia. cane can be bought at most tackle shops. Round cane is no good for stick floats. High density split cane must be used for these floats and tapered to suit. This can be obtained from gardening shops and is normally painted green. Cane from old broken split cane rods can also be utilised for this purpose.

Elder pith. This material is obtained in the winter months by cutting off the dead vertical branches from the elderberry trees. After drying out for a couple of weeks the outside casing of wood and bark is split away leaving the pith centre. This is a very fragile material. It is difficult to work and is easily damaged. This material can be used for making the bodies of Avon and antenna floats. I normally find that several liberal coatings of aircraft dope mixed with talcum powder will form a protective shell before painting. Elder pith floats are a dream to use but are not recommended for construction by beginners.

Inserts for antenna floats. These can be made from fine crowquill ends, plastic brush bristles, cocktail sticks, fine pieces of peacock, cane or fibreglass. They are used to fit a very fine sensitive tip into the top of peacock or sarkandas reed float stems, making several mm of tip sensitive to a small dust shot for amplifying lift bites or for cutting down wind resistance in choppy water.

These then are the main materials used in float making. I shall now go into the details of constructing most of the types of floats used in fishing still and flowing water. The materials I suggest are the correct balance of materials

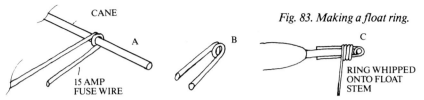

Fig. 83. Making a float ring.

proven over the years to be the most efficient. By all means experiment with different shapes of body and different lengths of stem later on, but for your first attempts at float making stick to the materials and specifications given, then you will not go far wrong and you will have a fully usable range of floats for most conditions. Also, you want to start as I have started with the easiest constructions first, then move onto the more complicated models later as your confidence and ability increases.

Almost all of the float designs I am about to show you have one thing in common, the float ring is whipped onto the float stem with whipping silk, so it is important to be able to carry out this operation efficiently before attempting to make your floats.

The float rings themselves are made by wrapping a piece of 15 amp fuse wire twice around a piece of thin cane or metal rod, pulling the ends tight to make a nice even ring. You then remove the rod and trim the ends off, leaving the two prongs about 10 mm to 12 mm long (see Fig. 83B). These are then placed either side of the float stem and whipped securely on (see Fig. 83C).

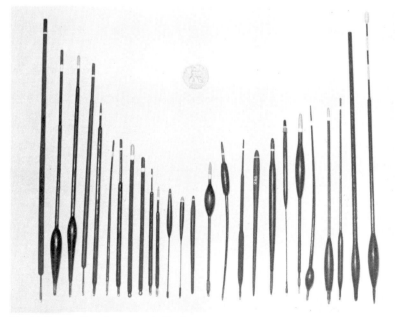

Fig. 84. Some of my home made floats.

The whipping on itself is very easy to do. It's the finishing of the whip that seems to be the difficult part. But once you have successfully done one, you will see that there is nothing difficult about it at all. Before you start to whip, cut about 6-8 inches of silk off the spool and lay it to one side. This will be your pullthrough for finishing the whip later on.

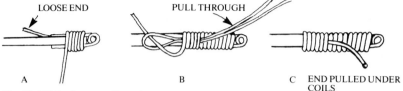

LOOSE END   PULL THROUGH

A   B   C   END PULLED UNDER
                                   COILS

Fig. 85. Whipping on a float ring.

Take the spool of silk and lay the silk along the float stem with the loose end pointing away from the eye. You then start to evenly wrap the silk around the float stem, ring prongs and loose end in neat even turns, making sure that each turn lays tightly up against each previous turn without crossing over it. When you have reached the end of your float ring prongs, do another couple of turns along the float stem. You then pick up the 6-8″ length of silk and double it over, lay this along your stem as shown in Fig. 85, with the loop pointing away from your previous whipping. Start to whip over the pullthrough and the float stem for another 5 or 6 turns, then cut the silk from the spool and thread the end through the loop of the pullthrough. Take hold of the two loose ends of the pullthrough and very carefully pull the loop under the last 5 or 6 coils of the whipping which at the same time will pull the loose end of the silk under the coils as well (see Fig. 85). This will trap the loose end under the coils giving it a neat finish. The excess can then be cut off as close to the coils as possible.

This is how you do a whip. The same method is used for whipping on rod rings, so if you master this you will have no problems when you come to repair or make your own rods.

Now for your first float. For this you need a crow or goose quill. You first of all need to remove the feather fibres from the quill. This is done by trimming off the fibres with a modelling knife or razor blade, cutting them off as close to the quill as possible, starting at the thick end and cutting towards the thin end, (see Fig. 86). Do not go the other way as this can cause the fibres to tear the protective skin away from the quill making it hard to smooth down and removing its natural water resistance. Do not try to cut the fibres off too closely to the quill as you may cut into the quill by accident. Any stubble can be removed with fine sandpaper afterwards.

BLADE →

Fig. 86. Stripping a quill.

After removing the feather fibres and trimming it to the length required, you need to smooth the quill down with fine sandpaper or wet and dry paper. Now take a close look at the quill at its thinnest part. You will see that it has a groove running all along one side. Opposite to the groove you will see that the other side is very hard and shiny. This is the backbone of the quill and you can use this to make the eye. Holding your quill with the groove uppermost, take your blade and cut into the soft part of the quill about 20 mm from the thinnest end, taking great care not to cut through the back bone, (see Fig. 87).

Fig. 87.

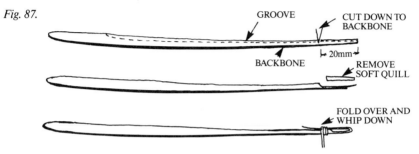

Then from the end of the quill, cut up towards this first incision, removing the soft waste quill. The hard piece of back bone can then be rubbed smooth and folded over forming an eye. You then whip it down to finish it off. You now have a very sensitive trotting float. It can be left in its natural colour with just a coat of varnish and the tip painted red or black, or you can paint the body any colour you wish before varnishing. This float is fished by connecting it to the line with float rubbers top and bottom for a quick change, or by passing the line through the eye and connecting it with a float rubber at the top (see Fig. 88).

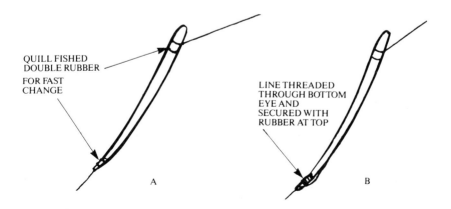

Fig. 88.

To make a sensitive float for still water, you can still use a similar quill, but this time, you can up end it (see Fig. 89). After dressing and smoothing the quill, you can whip an eye onto the thick end. If a self cocking float is required, you can whip an eye onto a short length of 16 s.w.g. brazing rod. Cut off the top 3 mm from the float and glue the rod into the base with Araldite (see Fig. 89). These floats are fished connected to the line by the bottom only.

Fig. 89.

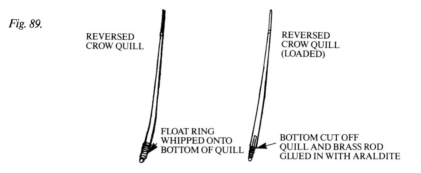

REVERSED
CROW QUILL

REVERSED
CROW QUILL
(LOADED)

FLOAT RING
WHIPPED ONTO
BOTTOM OF QUILL

BOTTOM CUT OFF
QUILL AND BRASS ROD
GLUED IN WITH ARALDITE

Now let's look at a simple waggler type float. This can be made from a straight piece of peacock or sarkandas reed. The float stem is drilled with a drill or a nail to take either 2 mm cane or 16 s.w.g. brass if loading is required. Always whip your ring onto the brass or cane before assembly, then the last part of your whipping will go inside the float on assembly, preventing any chance of the whipping coming undone (see Fig. 90).

Fig. 90.

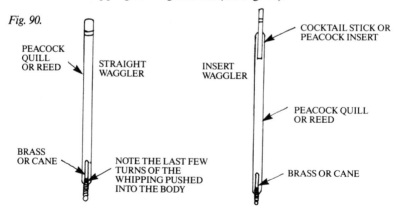

PEACOCK
QUILL
OR REED

STRAIGHT
WAGGLER

INSERT
WAGGLER

COCKTAIL STICK OR
PEACOCK INSERT

PEACOCK QUILL
OR REED

BRASS
OR CANE

NOTE THE LAST FEW
TURNS OF THE
WHIPPING PUSHED
INTO THE BODY

BRASS OR CANE

The floats can be made in sets from 4″-12″ long stepping up in size at 1″ intervals. For still waters, a fine insert made from a cocktail stick or thin piece of peacock can be fitted. Now let's look at the same floats but this time with the addition of a body.

If a body is added to the upper part of the quill float it makes an Avon type trotting float. If a body is added to a bird quill with the exception of peacock, it should be a cork body if proper balance is to be achieved. Balsa bodied Avon floats have a cane stem, (see Fig. 91). Note the position of the body in relation to the length of the quill or cane. The length of the body should not exceed ⅓ of the total float length. Otherwise the float will become unstable. Also it is always positioned about 20 mm from the top of the stem.

Fig. 91. Construction of Avon floats.

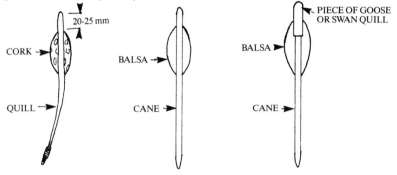

If you want a thick top on an Avon float to make it more visible when trotting long distances, this can be achieved without using thicker quill or cane stems. A piece cut from the end of a goose or swan quill can be inserted into the top of the body, (see Fig. 91) and glued into position.

If a body is fitted to the bottom of the bird quill or a cane stem, then this float is called a ducker. These are used for trotting flowing water in down stream wind conditions, (see Fig. 92).

Fig. 92. Duckers.

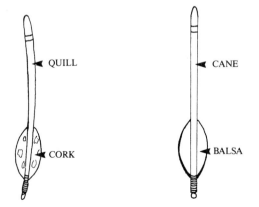

If a body is fitted to the bottom of a piece of peacock quill or sarkandas reed, a cane stem should be used to connect the quill or reed to the body. This makes a much stronger float than if the hole in the body is drilled right out to take the full diameter of the quill or reed (see Fig. 93). It also makes the assembly of the float much quicker and easier with less chance of damaging the quill.

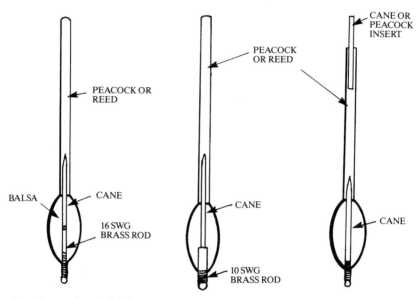

Fig. 93. Wagglers with balsa bodies.

If thin quill or reed is used then 2mm diameter cane will do. If thicker quill is used 3 mm diameter cane will be needed. If we want a loaded float, then either 16 s.w.g. or 10 s.w.g brass rod can be used together with the cane. These floats are called zoomers or missiles. As with the ordinary wagglers, tip inserts can be added if greater sensitivity is required.

Sometimes you may want very sensitive zoomers or antenna type floats with non-buoyant stems, this is so you can have a greater length of float tip showing above the water in windy or choppy conditions. In this case the stem made of cane or fibreglass is supported by a balsa body.

If you intend to fish at long range in choppy water then a balsa sight bulb can be fitted to the tip to allow you to see it better (see Fig. 94). Also the balsa bodies are longer to make the floats more stable due to their extra length of stem. Again if loading is required, these can be cane with the lower part made of brass rod. Old quiver tips can be used if fibreglass stems are required.

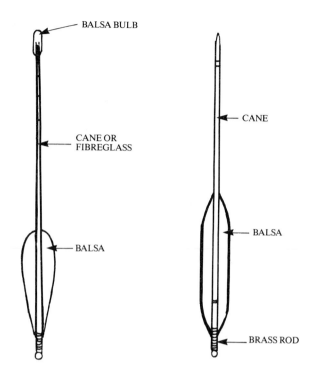

Fig. 94. Antenna floats.

If you intend to shape your own balsa bodies, always drill the balsa first before you start to shape it. It is very difficult to drill balsa dowell squarely without running off centre. Tube drills as opposed to spiral fluted drills are the best type to use on balsa wood. These can be made from old car aerials which are ideal for the job.

The next range of floats are the balsa trotting and stick floats. These floats are quite easy to make providing you take it easy with the shaping. This is the most difficult part, keeping the tapers symmetrical and even. Your first attempts will probably be way out of true, I know mine were. But after a bit of practice you will soon develop a trained hand and eye.

The most uncomplicated of the balsa floats to make is the simple trotting float. This can be made from either 6 mm or 8 mm dia. balsa dowel for a slim close range float, or from 10 mm or 15 mm dowel for the dumpy chub type trotters which we use for supporting large baits in fast flowing rivers (see Fig. 95).

147

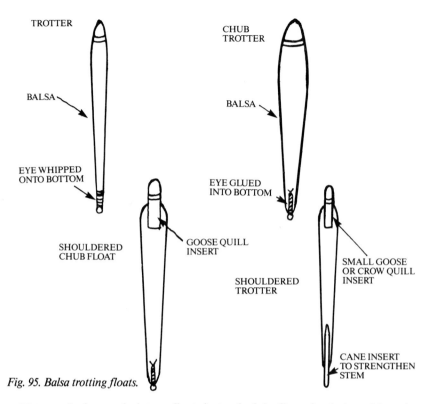

Fig. 95. Balsa trotting floats.

Note on the larger chub type float, instead of the float ring being whipped to the base of the float, the two prongs have been twisted together and then pushed into the base of the float and cemented in. A stronger bottom can be achieved by drilling the balsa before shaping it and glueing in a short piece of cane. The balsa can then be tapered down to give a nice smooth line.

Straight balsa floats do have a habit of riding up out of the water if held back. One way of overcoming this tendency is to make a shoulder below the tip. The water then will act on this shoulder, holding the float down. The best way of doing this is to drill and shape the balsa and then cement in a piece of quill. This will make a stronger top than if you try to form the shoulder and tip from solid balsa. It is also quicker and neater.

Now we come to the stick floats. These floats, as previously described, have a weighted bottom made of wire or high density cane. The tapers of the balsa can be either long at the top or long at the bottom. These are known as standard or reversed. A standard taper gives the float more stability, but the tip is less sensitive. This is ideal for medium to fast flows, but in slow moving water the reverse taper is more sensitive and the slight reduction in stability is not detrimental (see Fig. 96).

Note the proportions in the length of wire to balsa and the length of cane to balsa. With wire stemmed floats, the best stability is achieved with a proportion of 2/5 balsa to 3/5 wire with approximately 25 mm of wire inside the balsa. If 4 mm-6 mm balsa dowel is used the thin 22 gauge or 20 gauge wire is needed. For heavier floats using 8 mm to 10 mm dia. balsa, then 18 gauge wire is the size to use.

When making the traditional cane and balsa stick floats, ⅔ cane and ⅓ balsa is the correct proportion of material to use. The cane and balsa stick float is assembled and glued before shaping. These are always made with a standard taper. The balsa is tapered down to the width of the cane and the cane is then tapered down towards the bottom. No float ring is fitted to the base of a cane and balsa stick float. It is always fixed to the line with two pieces of silicone tubing to allow for a quick change of float.

Body lengths can vary from 30 mm in length upwards in steps of 5 mm. The stem lengths are then increased in the suggested ratios. Once a body length of 60 mm is reached, it is then advisable to go up in balsa diameter rather than increase the length of the body, when floats of a greater shot carrying capacity are needed. Otherwise the floats will be too long and awkward to cast and handle properly.

When painting your floats, one way of achieving a super smooth finish and sealing the float against any chance of water penetration, is to first paint on a mixture of model aircraft dope mixed with talcum powder. When dry, this can be smoothed down with very fine wet and dry paper and any slight irregularities will be filled and smoothed over. Also it will give your floats added strength.

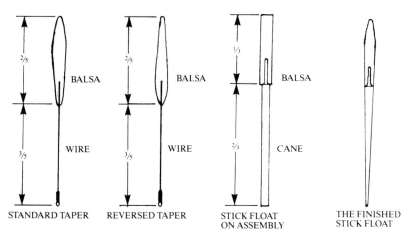

Fig. 96. Stick float construction.

After painting on your main colour, the float should then be given a coat of varnish before the tip of the float is painted. Varnish is best rubbed onto the float with your finger. Do not put it on too thickly or it will run and spoil the appearance of the float. If runs do occur, these can be sanded down with very fine wet and dry paper after the varnish has hardened off. It may only take a day for the varnish to dry, but it will take up to a week before it fully hardens, so a bit of care taken when applying the varnish can save a lot of time later on.

The best way to hang your floats whilst the paint or varnish is drying is to put your block of polystyrene onto a shelf and pin the floats through the float ring into the side of the block near the base (see Fig. 97).

When the varnish has dried, you can now put on the tip colour. Fluorescent colours need a white base before they can be applied. Normal matt white enamel can be used for this or proper white base paint can be used. The base white must be fully dry before the colour can be applied.

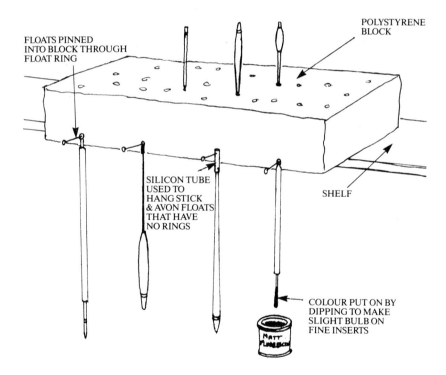

POLYSTYRENE BLOCK

FLOATS PINNED INTO BLOCK THROUGH FLOAT RING

SILICON TUBE USED TO HANG STICK & AVON FLOATS THAT HAVE NO RINGS

SHELF

COLOUR PUT ON BY DIPPING TO MAKE SLIGHT BULB ON FINE INSERTS

Fig. 97. Hanging floats to dry.

If the paint is thin the best way of colouring the tips is to dip them. On very fine tips this can be an advantage as the paint will dry with a slightly bulbous look at the end (see Fig. 97), enabling you to see it more clearly.

Always wash your paint brushes out with thinners or turps immediately after use. Store your tins of paint and varnish upside down. This will prevent a hard skin from forming on top of the paint in the tin. Make sure the lids are fitted on tightly.

Rod Building and Repairs

Modern rods made of hollow glass and carbon fibre are far easier to make than their old cane and wood predecessors. Most rod kits bought today have the joints ready fitted and all they require is the handle fitting on and the rings whipped into position. Some kits can be bought with the handles ready fitted and only the rings need whipping on and the finished rod varnishing. These normally cost a couple of pounds more than the basic kit, so it can pay you to learn how to fit and finish your own handles. It's far easier than it at first appears.

All you need are the right diameter corks, a round file, a tube of Bostik or Evo-stik, a roll of masking tape, some rough and smooth glasspaper and a sanding block. The sanding block is just a piece of wood around which you wrap your glass paper. Most blanks are parallel where the corks are fitted on (see Fig. 98). The corks come in different sizes and are graded by the size of their holes. Each cork is about 20 mm long, so two dozen or more are needed for the average rod. The corks should be a snug fit on the handle and not loose. If for example a No. 13 cork is too slack, then No. 12 corks will have to be used and the hole opened out slightly with the round file, or the masking tape is wrapped around the blank to take up the slackness in the holes. The corks are then pushed on to the handle and glued into position (see Fig. 98).

The corks now have to be sanded down until the reel fittings will just slide over. Do not try to sand down the whole length of the handle in one go. Remove the bulk of the excess cork and then finish off a couple of inches of the handle at a time, starting from the bottom end (see Fig. 99). The bulk of the excess cork is best removed with rough glass paper. As you near the required diameter, start using medium glass paper. Fine glass paper is then used to finish off and leave a smooth finish. Cork is very soft and easy to sand down. A pair of outside callipers and a straight edge are useful items to have to help you keep your sanding square and even to the blank. The top of the handle is tapered outwards to stop the reel fittings from sliding off up the rod (see Fig. 99).

The last half dozen corks are best left off until last, then when the handle has been sanded and the reel fittings slid on, these last few corks can then be glued on and blended into the handle, tapering outwards near the bottom to stop the reel fittings sliding off the end. We now have a partly built rod. The only job to do now is to position and whip on the rings.

The spacing of the rings is largely determined by the action of the rod. In a tip actioned rod, the spacing of the rings especially on the top joint, will be a lot closer than the spacing on a through action rod. This is to ensure that the line is made to follow the natural curve of the rod as close as possible, getting the maximum efficiency from the rods action. I have given some suggested ring spacings for rods of varying lengths and actions (see Fig. 100).

Fig. 98. Gluing corks to handle.

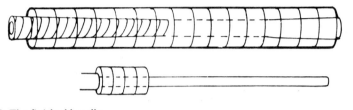

Fig. 99. The finished handle.

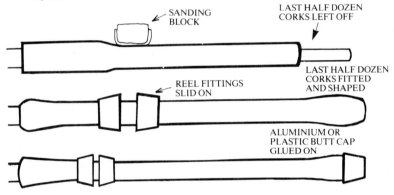

SANDING BLOCK

LAST HALF DOZEN CORKS LEFT OFF

REEL FITTINGS SLID ON

LAST HALF DOZEN CORKS FITTED AND SHAPED

ALUMINIUM OR PLASTIC BUTT CAP GLUED ON

Fig. 100. A guide to ring spacings.

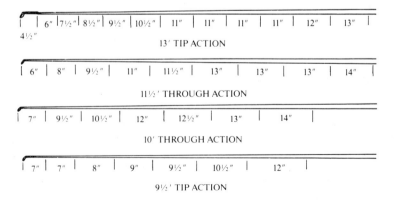

4½" | 6" | 7½" | 8½" | 9½" | 10½" | 11" | 11" | 11" | 11" | 12" | 13"

13' TIP ACTION

6" | 8" | 9½" | 11" | 11½" | 13" | 13" | 13" | 14"

11½' THROUGH ACTION

7" | 9½" | 10½" | 12" | 12½" | 13" | 14"

10' THROUGH ACTION

7" | 7" | 8" | 9" | 9½" | 10½" | 12"

9½' TIP ACTION

The more recent float and leger rods with test curves of 12 ozs have intermediate rings of the hard chrome stand off type, or the small Fuji aluminium oxide lined type. They are all of one size — Size 'O'. The butt ring is normally of the standard butt ring size, lined with aqualite or sintox ceramic. These 'O' rings have been proved to be superior to the old staggered sized rings in respect of casting distance and accuracy. Rods with a test curve of 1¼ lbs upwards use the stronger bridge type rings. Again these are plated with hard chrome. These are necessary to take the pressure put on them by the heavier lines and fish (see Fig. 101). They are also larger in diameter.

Fig. 101.

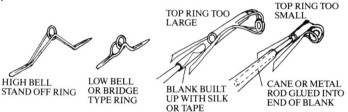

HIGH BELL
STAND OFF RING

LOW BELL
OR BRIDGE
TYPE RING

TOP RING TOO
LARGE

TOP RING TOO
SMALL

BLANK BUILT
UP WITH SILK
OR TAPE

CANE OR METAL
ROD GLUED INTO
END OF BLANK

Never glue the top ring onto the blank, otherwise if you need to replace it when it wears or gets damaged you will have to cut the rod tip off. If it is a slack fit, you can either cut the tip back, or build up the tip with whipping silk or masking tape (see Fig. 101).

When whipping an intermediate ring onto a rod blank, it is much easier if you fasten the ring to the rod with a piece of masking tape wrapped around one end. This keeps the ring in position and in line whilst the other end is being whipped on (see Fig. 102).

Fig. 102. Whipping on a ring.

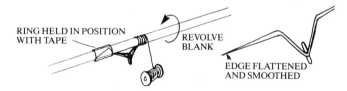

RING HELD IN POSITION
WITH TAPE

REVOLVE
BLANK

EDGE FLATTENED
AND SMOOTHED

The ends of the rings should also be flattened and dressed with a small hammer and file before fitting, otherwise it will be very difficult to get an even finish when you come to the edge if it is too steep. When whipping the ring on to the rod, revolve the rod rather than the spool of silk. This makes the job much easier and a tighter whip can be achieved. The whip is finished in the same way as described at the beginning of the chapter by using the pull through. The whippings can be sealed before varnishing by rubbing in model aircraft dope with your finger, revolving the rod in one direction as you do this to give you a smooth finish. This brings out the colour of the whipping and maintains it whilst varnishing. If this is not done the silk will soak up the varnish and darken in colour. When varnishing the rod, gloss or matt varnish can be rubbed onto the blank with your finger. Again care must be taken to coat it thinly or runs will develop, spoiling the finish of the rod.

If you are replacing a ring or all of the rings on an old rod, you must rub the rod down smoothly to remove all the old varnish. Fibreglass blanks can be painted if you wish to do so. This is best done using the aerosol paint used for car body work, but you must use an undercoat first. As with varnishing, this must be applied lightly or runs will develop. A piece of string trapped into the end of the blank with a wooden or cork plug will allow you to hang the blank whilst spraying and drying, (see Fig. 103). The cork handle can be masked with masking tape.

Fig. 103. Painting a rod.

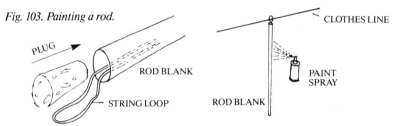

PLUG

ROD BLANK

STRING LOOP

ROD BLANK

CLOTHES LINE

PAINT SPRAY

Bank Sticks and Rod Rest Heads

These are made from non-rusting materials such as brass and aluminium. The drawings are self explanatory and easy to interpret. All these accessories have a standard thread ⅜ B.S.F. This is the same thread as used by the tackle manufacturers, so any shop bought accessories will fit your own items.

Let's look at a bank stick first.

This is made from a length of 12 mm diameter aluminium tube. One end is flattened and shaped into a point. A small rivet can be fitted near the point to stop the two pieces from opening out when it is pushed into the ground.

Onto the other end is fitted the brass cap drilled and tapped to ⅜ B.S.F. This is slid on to the end of the tube and held into place by being drilled and riveted. These can be made in lengths of 3-4 or 5 ft as required.

The rod rest head is made from 3 mm aluminium rod or cadmium coated steel rod, fitted through a 15 mm dia. brass or aluminium body that has been turned down and screwed to ⅜ B.S.F. This rod is then locked into position with a self tapping screw and the ends bent up as shown. Plastic tubing is fitted over the ends making a neat snag free rod rest head. They can be made in various lengths and a line vee can be made by sliding a loose piece of rod into the plastic tubing and bending it to the required shape before fitting it to the rod rest. This type of rod rest is used when free-lining or link legering, and allows the line to run through it without being trapped between the rod blank and the rod rest.

Fig. 104. Making a bank stick.

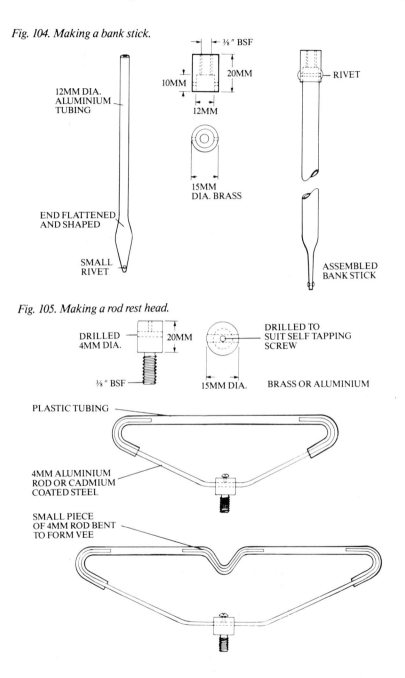

Fig. 105. Making a rod rest head.

Throwing Sticks
These can be made of plastic or aluminium tubing. A wooden or cork plug is pushed down the end and glued into position 35 mm-45 mm down the tube. The tube should be cut to a length of 18-20 inches and if metal tube is used, the bottom should be cut at an angle to allow it to be stuck into the bank for one handed loading. If plastic tube is used a hardwood spike can be fitted in the end. 25 mm to 35 mm dia. tube is ideal for loose feed, but one of 40 mm-50 mm dia. is required for ground baiting. The thicker throwing sticks need not be that size all the way down. A cup can be fitted onto a turned down handle (see Fig. 106).

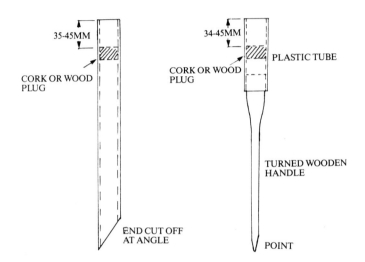

Fig. 106. Making a throwing stick.

Bite Indicators
These are very expensive to buy for what they are and can be made very cheaply. Some parts like the screws and the rings may need to be bought from the tackle shop, but they are only a fraction of the cost of the finished item. In the case of the swing tip, the rings can be made by cutting up and bending safety pins as no pressure is put on these rings by the line when playing fish.

To make a swingtip, all you need is an 8-10″ piece of 3 mm or ⅛″ dia. cane. Onto one end you whip on a bent safety pin and bend another safety pin into a shape that resembles a stand off rod ring. This is then whipped on, two-thirds of the way up the cane. The end of the cane is sanded down to a slight taper onto which is slid the silicon tubing link (see Fig. 107). A swing tip screw is then fitted into the end to complete the assembly, which can be painted black with a band of fluorescent paint on the tip if required.

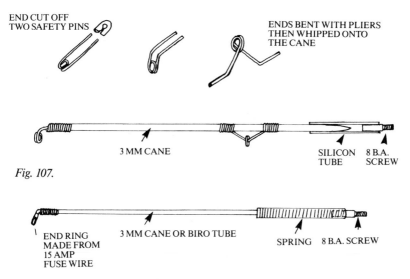

Fig. 107.

Fig. 108. Making a swingtip and springtip.

Never have more than a 10 mm gap between the end of the cane and the screw in the silicon tubing, otherwise the tip will be prone to back tangles whilst casting or playing fish.

Springtips
A very sensitive springtip can be made using a ball point pen spring, the plastic biro tube or 3 mm dia. cane, plus the inevitable screw. The tip ring can be made from either a safety pin as with the swing tip or 15 amp fuse wire as used for float rings (see Fig. 108). Stronger springs can be bought from model shops or ironmongers. The sensitivity of the tip can also be altered by the length of the cane or tube. No more than 6 mm of loose spring should be left between the tube or cane and the screw, otherwise the tip will sag and be too floppy.

Bobbin Indicators
Good bobbin indicators can be made by using the tops from washing-up liquid bottles. Mud or groundbait can be pushed into the ends if heavy bobbins are needed for fishing flowing water (see Fig. 109). Hairgrips make very good indicators if you prefer that the indicator should be struck off when the rod is lifted. Aluminium foil can be stuck on to the hairgrip to increase the visibility. This foil shows up quite well at night too, but if you can afford them, then Beta lights can be aradited on (see Fig. 110). A 2 ft length of nylon or string is attached to the end and is fastened into the ground by a metal tent peg. When the rod is lifted to strike the clip of the hairgrip is pulled off of the line.

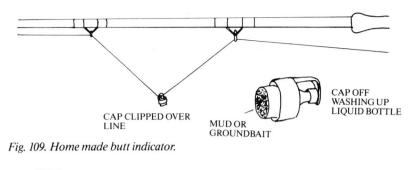

CAP CLIPPED OVER
LINE

MUD OR
GROUNDBAIT

CAP OFF
WASHING UP
LIQUID BOTTLE

Fig. 109. Home made butt indicator.

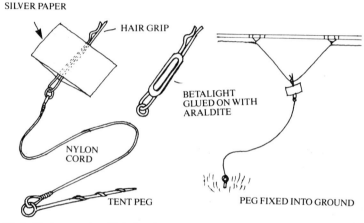

SILVER PAPER

HAIR GRIP

BETALIGHT
GLUED ON WITH
ARALDITE

NYLON
CORD

TENT PEG

PEG FIXED INTO GROUND

Fig. 110. Indicators made with hair grips.

Tackle Boxes

A good strong tackle carrier and seat can be made from 6 mm or ¼ " plywood
fitted to a wooden frame made of 25 mm square pine. It need not be jointed, it
can be simply screwed and dowelled together. The lid can be made of thicker
plywood to give more support for your weight, but this is not necessary if you
are just a lightly built person. Vinyl covered foam can be fitted onto the lid to
give extra comfort. Slots can be cut out in the side panels to allow the strap to
pass through. The lid can be secured by a simple hasp and staple held closed by
a tapered peg. This peg can be connected to the box by a length of nylon string
which is fastened to the box by a small nut and bolt or a screw.

Small fishing baskets are now approaching the same cost as a good budget
priced rod or mid price range reel. So any money saved in making your own
box can be channelled into purchasing these more important items.

Boxes for carrying small items of tackle such as floats, hooks, swingtips and shot, can also be made quite cheaply. Again plywood can be used for the main part of the box, but redwood should be used for the partitioning pieces. The more complex type has a removable tray into which holes are drilled to take your tubs of shot. Hook boxes can be stored under this tray, keeping them covered away from sudden showers of rain. A simple float box, using slotted foam is also easy to make. This can be incorporated on top of the tackle box to give you a double tier box, the bottom of the float compartment being used to form the lid of the tackle compartment. Slotted foam can be bought from most good tackle shops.

All these boxes should be given several good coats of varnish before use to stop them warping with the damp, or holding moisture in the wood, which can cause your tackle and hooks to corrode.

These then are a few of the many items of tackle you can make yourself. The money you save can be used to buy better quality items such as rods, reels, and nets etc, and a great deal of pleasure will be gained by using tackle of your own design and making. Also, by making your own items, a greater knowledge of how they work and function will be learned. This will help you overcome many of the problems of catching fish in difficult situations that you will come up against in your angling career.

17 SAFETY HINTS

Many of the waters you are likely to fish will be shallow or well populated, and an occasional soaking caused by the bank giving way or by your basket toppling over will be greeted with cheers and laughter by your companions, and very little damage other than to your pride will have been done.

There are many occasions though, when fishing alone or when fishing deep lakes or fast flowing rivers where the banks are steep, when a tumble into the water could cost you your life.

Even if you are an excellent swimmer, and it is important to learn how to swim if you intend to take your angling seriously, the fact that you are probably wearing heavy clothing and waders will make it very difficult for you to reach the bank again due to your clothes becoming waterlogged and being caught against the force of the current. A trip or stumble on a remote stretch of water, especially in the winter months, can leave you stranded on a deserted bank either unconscious or with a broken leg. You will be then at the mercy of the elements and you could die of exposure before you are found.

It is therefore very important when fishing alone, to tell someone at home exactly where you are going and when you will be likely to come home.

These then are just a couple of examples of what might happen, and why I consider it important to include this chapter in this book. Also, why it is important that you should read it and absorb it. By being aware, you can take steps to prevent yourself from being caught up in any dangerous situations.

Most of these safety hints are common sense, and you will probably think of a few more that are particularly appropriate to your local waters.

1. Before leaving home, make sure you are adequately dressed to keep warm and dry if the weather conditions deteriorate whilst you are fishing.

2. Make sure someone at home knows where you are going to fish and at what time you are likely to get home.

3. If you are going on your bicycle, make sure your tackle is secure and will not swing round and pull you off balance. Make certain that your rods or holdall are well clear of the wheels. Should they get caught in your spokes, they could fetch you off of your bike into the path of another vehicle. At best it could result in your rods being broken beyond repair.

4. When choosing your swim, make sure you are well clear of any steep or slippery banks, or places where the bank overhangs the water and has been undercut by the current. This could collapse under your weight throwing you and your tackle into the water.

5. Position your basket so that it is level and stable and well clear of the waters edge. Use a trowel if necessary to do this.

6. If fishing on a tidal stretch of water make sure that you can safely and quickly move your tackle up the bank as the water level rises, or if a barge comes down the river leaving a large wash in its wake.

7. Never lay rods or tackle behind you on the bank, especially in crowded areas or where cattle can get down to the bankside.

8. Position all your nets and tackle so that everything can be reached without having to get up off your basket or seat.

9. Never wade unless it is essential and only then when you have tested the depth of the water and the firmness of the bottom with your landing net handle.

10. Avoid all high walls or banks especially near weirs or lockgates.

11. Never walk along the tops of weirs or waterfalls. They are very slippery due to silk weed and erosion.

12. Do not be tempted to wade out to islands or sand bars, especially in tidal rivers and in the upper reaches of spate rivers. These waters can rise 5 or 6 feet in a matter of minutes due to tides, or rain storms in their upper reaches.

13. Do not use makeshift rafts or boats to fish out in lakes or rivers. Especially if they are deep or fast flowing. If you use a boat, make sure you know what you are doing.

14. Never walk on to the frozen surface of a pond, lake or river.

15. Take a great care if you climb a tree to retrieve lost tackle or to spot fish. Avoid any thin or dead looking branches, especially if these overhang the water.

16. Never go night fishing alone. Always go with a companion and do not go walking around unfamiliar areas of the waterside in the dark. You may trip or fall and you could either break a leg or knock yourself unconscious. Remember, if unconscious you could drown in just 2 inches of water if you fall face downwards.

17. When fishing in country areas be very careful when crossing fields. Make sure you close all gates and keep a sharp lookout for notices warning you of bulls. A lot of jokes are told about bulls, but believe me they can and do kill unwary people. You will be unable to run if laden down with heavy tackle.

18. Never fish dangerous waters alone. Tidal rivers and fast flowing rivers, deep lakes with high or slippery banks, canal towpaths without safety chains are all areas that should be avoided unless accompanied by someone who is big enough or strong enough to help if accidents should arise.

19. If a companion or anyone else falls into the water, by all means help. But do not risk your own life by any rash actions. Try to reach them by using your landing net or a branch. If they are out of reach look for something large

and buoyant to throw out to them such as a life belt, oil drum or football. When fishing a canal or park lake, always make a note of where any lifebelts are situated.

20. Never enter the water to help someone in trouble unless you are a very strong swimmer and you have first removed all your heavy outer clothing. Take advantage of any life saving classes at your local swimming baths. It could save your own life as well as someone elses.

21. When casting in crowded areas such as parks or roadside stretches of water, take great care not to endanger passers by. Keep all large treble hooks and gaff points covered with cork when not in use.

18 WATERSIDE CODE

Angling is a very pleasant sport and it relies a lot on the manners and good will between its participants and the owners of the waters and surrounding land for its success. The knowledge and practice of the country code and waterside code is important if the sport is to be maintained and the facilities increased.

The leaving of litter and the subsequent injuries to livestock and wild life has been the biggest contributory factor to the loss of fishing rights over the last couple of years.

As far as young anglers are concerned, many waters have shut their doors to juniors due to disruptive behaviour by the youngsters, who when bored by their lack of success, have diverted their activities away from the pursuit of catching fish and have used the banks of the water as a general playground, much to the annoyance of the senior anglers whose sport has been spoilt by youngsters running up and down the banks shouting and throwing sticks and stones and generally making themselves a nuisance.

It is important if help and knowledge is to be obtained from the older anglers, to behave and conduct yourselves in a responsible manner. Even so, bad behaviour at the waterside is not solely confined to the young anglers. Many senior anglers are just as guilty in certain aspects of conduct as are the younger lads, and many a bad example is set by these senior anglers in front of young anglers whose code of conduct up to that time was impeccable.

It is, therefore important to learn and put into practice good waterside conduct and not be disillusioned by the behaviour of your fellow anglers, young or old, who are less well mannered and as thoughtful as yourselves.

It is much better that they learn from you, rather than allow yourselves to follow their bad example. Also, by practicing your code, you will increase your own chances of catching fish and gain more pleasure from your sport than they will.

Here then are the golden rules that make a responsible angler:

1. Always approach the water quietly. Never walk along the edge of the bank or along the skyline.

2. Never leave your cycles or vehicles blocking gates or lanes.

3. Close all gates and never break down hedges and fences.

4. Never trespass. Keep to the proper footpaths and access points.

5. Do not tread down crops or stray across farmland.

6. Always, before fishing, make sure you have the proper licences and permits. Observe all notices concerning boundaries and bye-laws.

7. Keep well down and tread softly when approaching other anglers.

8. Do not take transistor radios or cassette players to the waterside.

9. Never leave any litter, loose line or used shot by the waterside.

10. Do not use unnecessary lights when night fishing, and never allow them to flash or shine across the water.

11. Never light fires under any circumstances.

12. Never break down or destroy the bankside growth or cover.

13. Never shout or call out loudly. Do not run along the banks.

14. If using a boat or punt, keep well clear of the bank and areas of water being fished by anglers on the bank.

15. Never interfere with or spoil any other anglers pleasure.

16. Never go fishing without a hook disgorger.

17. Never leave a baited rod unattended.

19 GUIDE TO ANGLING LAW

It is important that all anglers know something about angling administration and the laws which govern our sport.

The licensing system is very complex and unless something is known about it, anglers could find themselves in serious trouble. Ignorance has no defence in law and it is the duty of all anglers young or old to obey the bye laws of the Water Authority and the rules of their clubs and associations. Otherwise they are likely to lose their rights to fish and put their clubs or associations in jeopardy of losing their leases.

The Water Authorities

These are the organisations that control all our waters. The quality of the water, the maintenance of the waterways, and banks are all controlled by the Water Authority. Rod licences are issued by these authorities and it is illegal to go fishing without one once the minimum age at which a licence is necessary has been reached. The age limit can vary from area to area, so you must check with your tackle dealer from whom the licences are obtained what age limit is applicable to your respective area. On the back of the licence will be printed a summary of the bye laws. These must be read carefully and obeyed.

Once you have bought a rod licence, you are only authorised to use a single rod and line in that particular Water Authority area. IT IS NOT A PERMIT TO FISH ANY WATER IN THAT AREA.

The fishing rights of waters are controlled by either the land owners or the Water Authority and these are normally rented or leased to local angling clubs and associations.

It is necessary to purchase a season permit or a day permit from these clubs or associations before you are allowed to fish. Some waters are for season permit holders only and others can be fished with a day permit. Others are strictly private and are controlled by either syndicates or private clubs, membership of which is strictly controlled and must be obtained before being allowed to fish.

There are some stretches of water controlled by the Water Authority, where licence holders can fish without first obtaining a permit. Your local tackle dealer can advise you about these. Other stretches controlled by the Water Authority require the purchase of a day or season permit in addition to the rod licence before you are allowed to fish.

Angling Organisations. The Association

Local clubs are normally affiliated to one or more local associations. This is to allow club members to fish association waters in addition to their own club waters. The facilities of the associations are used by the clubs for booking local matches or when help and advice is needed by the club in respect of stocking policies and legal problems. If the association is unable to deal with a particular problem then this is refered to one of the national angling bodies to which most large associations are also affiliated.

The National Anglers Council

The N.A.C. is recognised by the Minister of Sport and the Sports Council as the responsible body representing the whole of the sport of angling.

(a) Its objects are to co-operate with its members in encouraging the promotion and development of the sport of angling in England and Wales amongst all sections of the community.

(b) To co-ordinate and put forward the views of all the bodies and persons concerned with the sport in England and Wales, in any negotiations or on any other appropriate occasion.

(c) To formulate and review an Anglers National policy.

It does not seek to govern the sport in the sense of laying down rules e.g. for size limits, tackle, allocation of water etc. It exists to improve the status of anglers in negotiations with the Government, to increse the supply of water for angling and to protect the interests of all anglers against the ever increasing threats of encroachment by other sports or pastimes.

The founder members of the N.A.C. are the National Federation of Anglers, the Salmon and Trout Association, The National Federation of Sea Anglers and the Fishmongers Company.

Membership is open to all angling clubs, associations and individuals.

The National Federation of Anglers

The N.F.A. is the organisation which represents Britain's coarse fishermen. Its objects are to promote measures for improving the laws relating to fisheries, to safeguard anglers rights, to fight pollution and abstraction and to encourage the protection and development of fisheries.

A founder member of the N.A.C. the N.F.A. also works directly with Water Authorities and the Ministry of Agriculture, Fisheries and Food, on all matters affecting coarse fishing.

The N.F.A. is organised into eight regions, each with its own regional council and secretary. Each council elects one representative to serve on the National Executive.

The N.F.A. also organises the National Angling Championships, the DAIWA/D.F.D.S. challenge competition and the Tuborg cup series.

Membership of the N.F.A. is open to all clubs and associations.

The Anglers Co-operative Association

The A.C.A. is an anti-pollution organisation which uses its members subscriptions to protect their waters. If necessary, it fights legal cases on behalf of its members under the Common Law, by seeking to obtain injunctions to restrain polluters from causing further pollution, together with obtaining damages.

Since it was founded in 1948, it has won many famous legal actions, stopped pollution on hundreds of miles of river and on many lakes, and has obtained hundreds of thousands of pounds in damages for its members.

Membership is open to all angling clubs and associations, to private individuals including juniors and to hotels, tackle dealers, manufacturers etc.

These are the main administrative bodies concerned with our sport. They put in many thousands of hours work, a lot of which is on a voluntary basis, to uphold the interests of anglers and improve the quality of our sport.

READER NOTES

DATE:	VENUE:	REMARKS